# THE DUSK OF MANKIND AND THE DAWN OF THE KINGDOM

HUGH J. HARMON

# Hugh J. Harmon

# THE DUSK OF MANKIND AND THE DAWN OF THE KINGDOM

Published by **K**INGDOM **B**OOK & **G**IFT LLP
P.O. Box 291975
Columbia, SC 29229
803-736-2472
www.kingdombookandgift.com

All rights reserved.
Written permission must be secured from the publisher
or author to use or reproduce any part of this book.

Copyright © 2007 by Hugh J. Harmon

Unless otherwise indicated, all Scripture quotations are taken from
the King James Version of the Bible. Copyright © 1994, 1997, by
World Bible Publishers, Inc. Used by permission of
World Bible Publishers, Inc. All rights reserved.

Scripture quotations marked Amplified or AMP are taken from the
Amplified Version of the Bible. Copyright © 1996, 1998.
Used by permission.

ISBN 978-0-6151-7273-6
Printed in the United States of America

# The Dusk of Mankind and the Dawn of the Kingdom

# TABLE OF CONTENTS

| | | |
|---|---|---|
| **Preface** | | 05 |
| **Introduction** | | 07 |
| **Chapter 1** | Facing the Facts | 12 |
| **Chapter 2** | Overcoming the giant named FEAR | 28 |
| **Chapter 3** | Running on Empty | 44 |
| **Chapter 4** | Lest We Stumble | 62 |
| **Chapter 5** | Developing a Deliberate Spirit | 76 |
| **Chapter 6** | Rebel, with a cause | 94 |
| **Chapter 7** | Declare Civil War | 116 |
| **Chapter 8** | Letting Go | 128 |
| **Chapter 9** | The Great Challenge | 152 |
| **Chapter 10** | Living in your midnight | 172 |
| **Chapter 11** | Advancing the Kingdom | 188 |
| **Chapter 12** | Kingdom Living in a Dying World | 216 |

## Hugh J. Harmon

*Dedicated to*
*The glory of God,*
*the great sacrifice He made,*
*and the sons and daughters*
*who are being repositioned*
*to see His glory.*

# The Dusk of Mankind and the Dawn of the Kingdom

## PREFACE

As the glory of God breaks through the dark horizon of human existence we await the shining forth of a marvelous light.  It is a light that bears within its very core the source of everlasting life.  It is a light that man has sought either to draw near to in hope and joy, or strove to escape in fear and doubt from the dawning of time.  This very same light has been in the possession of those who've been found to be faithful in not only protecting that light but in sharing that light with others.  They have shared that light literally and figuratively through acts of love, through retelling of their testimonies and through exuberant expressions of their gratefulness.

As we stand on the edge, I daresay the very brink of what I believe to be the greatest days of our lives may you too see this light, have opportunities to share in this light and in the end become enlightened.  The Bible says in the book of Hebrews, "For the word of God is quick and powerful, and sharper than any two-edged sword, piercing even to the dividing asunder of soul and spirit, and of the joints and marrow, and is a discerner of the thoughts and intents of the heart."  The light of which I speak is the light that comes from the Word of God, and it possesses this same power of the Word to lay bare all that we are, and all that we even contemplate or desire to become.  We may see our lot as hopeless if it continues on the course that we currently have to cope with, or we may see that our only hope is to step on others and survive as we best see fit.  However, the mentality of hopelessness or survival of the fittest or by any means necessary are man devised thought patterns, and man's time to amble along aimlessly causing more harm than help is just about over. Jesus, after being asked by His disciples how should they pray, and how should they address a God who wanted to reconnect with them even in their fallen state to build them back up by working through them, replied in this way. He said, "After this manner therefore pray ye: Our Father which art in heaven, hallowed be thy name. Thy kingdom come. Thy will be done on earth, as it is in heaven."

Let us call, and cause the kingdom of God to come to pass in this earth, in our time. Be blessed...

# The Dusk of Mankind and the Dawn of the Kingdom

## INTRODUCTION

With every passing generation, as far as recorded human history is concerned, there has been both natural and man-made cataclysmic change. These changes, be they political, societal or physical in nature, have all in their own way caused man to be introspective. Man's introspection has often led to ideations on the existence of God, on our purpose in this world, and on the possibility that human ability and potential is far greater than we can even comprehend. Our introspection has not only led to ideations on where we fit into the grand scheme of things but it has also led to many questions. These questions are based on contemplations about how we compare to other creatures. They are about whether we really are in control, an idea that we love to espouse either as guardians of nature or conversely of human concerns. They are questions about the reality of God. They are about whether God is just a figment of the collective imaginations of an imperfect people looking for perfect consistency in something outside of themselves. As we can see human thought vacillates between two polar extremes; with most of us occupying the center of a bell curve of sorts when it comes to our understanding of God and man. Either God exists for some us and He is in control, or He doesn't, and we somehow are ambling along unconsciously in control of our own destinies.

World history viewed from the parameters of human interference, and effect however, paints a rather gloomy picture concerning man's ability to improve his lot on his own. That makes the assessment that God doesn't exist and us running the show as a solo act, seem like an extreme position to hold. But, nevertheless, the debate goes on among the scientifically-minded secularist and the intellectually-astute believer over whether the human condition of division, predisposition to evil and the inability to improve the lives of all human beings is due to the fact that this world and our very lives are not our own. The scientist proposes that there are no ownership rights to be established. He says that we just happened to arrive on the scene by the natural outcomes of chemical evolution, just like the earth *came* to exist. The Christian on the other hand must believe that the world and their lives are both property of another, and this other has given us temporary ownership first of ourselves and lastly, of this earth.

Therefore, a dichotomous struggle develops in the psychology surrounding the understanding we have of our existence. Wars, national and international conflicts, ethnic rivalries, political upheaval and even natural disasters many times brings human beings to such disparate conclusions about who they are, and the power they have over their condition it is difficult to even imagine that this planet at the beginning of recorded and biblically-supported history was deeded to men. It was transferred in a contractually bound agreement to humankind.

The question now becomes whose fault is it that we are in the state that we are in? Additionally, we should ask what is the destiny of this earth under the control of humanity? As always I believe the best approach that can be undertaken to address these issues is to consult the biblical record. Understanding where we came from, why we came and to what ends we are ultimately heading requires that we do some biblical study and soul searching of the creator's intent for us. If we ascribe to a creator it would make the most sense to consult his record of the circumstances surrounding

# The Dusk of Mankind and the Dawn of the Kingdom

our creation. There is no better way to determine purpose in a things existence than to refer to the maker's manual. The Bible, the Word of God, is our maker's manual penned and lettered by scribes who worked under his watchful tutelage and guidance. You have got to believe that the Word of God is godly inspired before any of what I am about to say would even take root. Encased in the pages of Holy Writ is a treasure of knowledge about us that transcends even what the best textbooks may include about the anatomy and physiology of man.

The Dusk of Mankind, and the Dawn of the Kingdom of God, is a book that addresses, postulates and presents the concept of an irrevocable changing of the guard in earthly authority. The bedrock of the Bible is that almost immediately after this world was deeded to men as a temporary possession, the deed was thwarted by a relentless enemy. In man's greed to grasp after the straws of false knowledge that this enemy presented and because of his artful deception humanity forfeited the gift of the kingdom of this world to the prince of deception.

*The heaven, even the heavens, are the Lord's: but the earth hath he given to the children of men.*
Psalm 115:16

Man has ever since been in a tug-o-war with the devil, his own sin nature and his spirit man's desire to reconnect with God.

We stand today at the threshold of the dusk of man's forfeiture of the world and the dawn of the rebirth of the Kingdom. The premise of redemption in Jesus Christ, the crux of the bible, is that the sinless, life of Christ sacrificed through the crucifixion was the wage necessary to be paid unto God to win back not only man, but all that man had loss to the devil. The message of Jesus from the very start was, "Repent, for the kingdom of God is at hand!" He declared that man needed to turn away from some things and turn toward righteousness because the dominion of his father was near. Jesus knew that He bore in his very spirit the power, person and purpose of God to come near once again to His people. Disobedience, sin and misdirection had driven us out of His reach. Our sin obligated His desertion of us but even in that God envisioned a way for our return. He had mercy and approached us. Our intent was tainted by the dark attributes of greed, and disobedience and God calls us back to Him through Jesus. Jesus came bearing light to shred any remnant of darkness that lays within us.

The sun sets on man's failures and it rises on God's success through Jesus Christ. Join me in this thoughtful exhortation as I turn from all that's going wrong in my life and in this world, to all that God is doing right and getting ready to make manifest in the earth realm. Turn with me and look over the horizon as God's kingdom comes.

# The Dusk of Mankind and the Dawn of the Kingdom

## Chapter One

## Facing the Facts

As we log onto the latest news blog or flip through the pages of a national or local daily newspaper it is difficult to miss the bleak assemblage of disasters, crises and problems plaguing everyday American life. Ostensibly, we sit in a world ambling from peril to peril, and with the constant cry of, "What has befallen us?" Divisiveness and contention even among peer groups is quietly becoming the norm; as families are being devastated by parental abuse, adolescent and teenage waywardness, divorce and dissolution of the nuclear family. Our society is slowly but surely becoming a patchwork or an amalgam of non-traditional arrangements between men and women, co-habituating same-sex relationships, and a plurality of variations of the same. While the last gasping vestiges of traditional male-female unions consummated both legally and spiritually in the parameters of Godly marriage are all but obsolete, and are often labeled exceptions to the rule.

The rule appears to be that of temporary convenience over eternal covenant. The rule seems to suggest that deception and mistrust are normal, even acceptable character traits of a developing human psyche. Almost daily guilt and innocence in an act of criminal violence are both set aside for the tacit suggestion of mental incapacitation. The surest defense has become that of temporary, forced and irrepressible insanity. I did what I did because my mind was under the influence of some other agent or agency of which I had no control. Crime, which is really an aggravated, willful act of sin, is with every passing generation being medically diagnosed, offered a clinical label and increasingly being blamed on some genetic anomaly.

Disease and death seems to be reaching an alarming level in this generation. Ailments and causal practices that lead to physical affliction seems to be reaching record numbers between all age groups. Social status no longer is a determining factor when it comes to people getting infected with certain illnesses. There are no longer purely illnesses distinct to the lower class for example. The playing field on which the rat race of human experience is being engaged is being leveled by the apparent onslaught of the results and repercussions of years of poor lifestyle choices. Additionally, economic strain caused by errant consumption, uncontrolled borrowing and unilateral mismanagement of resources has placed our country in a quandary, unable to fulfill one of the central tenets of our governmental system and crippled in its ability to meet the constitutional obligations of ensuring the general public welfare. Healthcare costs have skyrocketed with the charlatan practices of fraudulent insurance subscribers. Doctors and other medical professionals fearful of legal recourse due to perceived medical malpractice have unavoidably raised the price of their services in an effort to curtail the expense of any future lawsuits that may be levied against them. The common thread of deception and greed are being neatly knit into the fabric of our society.

*And ye shall hear of wars, rumors of wars: see that you be not troubled: for all these things must come to pass, but the end is not yet. For nation shall rise against nation, and kingdom against kingdom: and there shall be famines, and pestilences, and earthquakes, in divers places. All these are the beginning of sorrows.*
Matthew 24:6-8

Again the question of what has befallen us resonates across the common conscience. The disaster and devastation during and in the aftermath of Hurricane Katrina left our nation cringing, and had some factions of society courting ideologies of color and class discrimination long thought to be buried in the ash heap of American southern history. The citizenry of the eighth ward in the parish of New Orleans, Louisiana even today feel slighted, neglected and disenfranchised by a national government consumed and over-extended with the ravages of a protracted war; and a local government immersed in inefficiency and the blame game, as if fearful of some community reprisal.

Foreign invasion to combat terrorism has gone through two subsequent metamorphoses. They first developed into rumors of war against foreign insurgency. Then eventually evolved into a full-blown life claiming, possibly draft inducing bloodshed. What we are facing is real. The issues and the problems that confront us each day are real. Most Americans are

# The Dusk of Mankind and the Dawn of the Kingdom

living not only above their means but actually are living on borrowed money and more evasively on borrowed time. The fact that we are unable as a collective group of people to hold on to the financial means to make life work for us, as we would like it, is real. There used to be an illusory teaching among general American philosophical banter that the realities of debt, inflation and a flagging social structure were myths of a paranoid, insecure public and hence baseless. That thought pattern immersed us in a depression some years ago that almost thoroughly devastated the American dream ideal of life being a flowery bed of ease. Wanton, exuberant spending led to the scourge of poverty and unfortunately the success of American enterprise ever since the depression has clouded our mind set, almost lifting us proverbially back into the clouds when it comes to fearlessness about our country's economic stability. Divorcing ourselves from reality at the expense of true freedom and sanity was never a viable option in the battle to face the facts of a challenging life. Yet still the entertainment and celebrity intoxicated under-culture of this world has managed to take center-stage, and interposed its will, as it were, on the American public consciousness. It has done this by offering almost a placebo-like relief from the pain of reality with the telecast of fabricated reality television. The new drug for calming the craziness of an ordinary unfulfilled life is to live vicariously through the experience of either the fame or the shame of others. But what do we do when the power goes out and when we have to close our eyes and live with the thoughts of personal disappointment haunting us.

    Natural disaster competes headlong with unnatural devastation. The dawning of the twenty-first century for this nation was not heralded with the popping of champagne and the dropping of the Tiffany crystal enlaced ball on New York's Time Square on New Year's Eve but rather was marked by a much more sinister occurrence in the very same city several months later.  The terrorist attacks of September 11, 2001 coined as a godless act upon an innocent and godly nation only initiated a domino effect that catapulted American society into a state of paranoia of which affect we still experience and endure today.  This paranoia for a moment triggered ethnic profiling in our airports and created a culture of vigilante justice that damaged the delicate relationship that already existed between the general American public and those within our borders who looked like the hijackers of that fateful day.  The Muslim faith was consequently put at odds with American patriotism.  And the God of Christianity was put under public scrutiny for allowing such a tragedy to happen within our homeland.

    As I sit to write these lines Americans are once again trying to put the pieces together from an act of home grown terror.  Students, staff and associated families of Virginia Tech University's 33 shooting victims are still wrestling with the tragedy of apparent misplaced anger.  The American collective is again dealing with, innocence under attack.  Thoughts on this latest violent tragedy have taken us back to the experience of the Oklahoma City bombing and the Atlanta Olympic bombing – reopening wounds.

    Debt and financial unfulfillment are probably the most pervasive predicaments that fuel despair in our society today.  Worldwide humanitarian efforts to curb the scourge of poverty and hunger; real or perceived, not only in America but also throughout the third world have become more prevalent.  But like the war that was declared on illegal drugs in the early 80s—the media

# The Dusk of Mankind and the Dawn of the Kingdom

coverage may have come to a standstill but the battle, the conflict and the problem still exists and persists. Unemployment and under-employment in our urban low-income communities continues to be an ever-present issue that does not seem to waiver regardless of the economic and political maneuvers made by each changing administration. The middle class; hard working, blue collar, middle-management, reliable types once shielded from the economic woes of a vacillating market due to the security bubble of a satisfactory credit score or standing, have now been immersed in the pool of depreciation with the current home foreclosure, sub-prime mortgage melt down and general decay of the credit system. Where does the solution lie? Who has the power and the authority to "deliver the goods"?

The facts in their totality are demonstrably glaring. All news seems to be unevenly weighed on the side of darkness and evil. The skies are a grim gray abstract of the blue that we once knew. The sun appears to be snuffed out but somewhere deep in the corner recesses of your conscience you see a slither of shining light. The light you see despite the enveloping darkness is the light of hope. There's something peculiar about hope, and that peculiarity lies in the fact that hope like light is strongest and most powerful when it is faced with its greatest adversity and opposition. What is hope if it is not standing toe to toe with a daunting oppositional challenge? What is light if it is not put to the test in the most extreme darkness?

This is the message of the gospel of the kingdom. The Bible prophetically declares in the book of Isaiah, in the ninth chapter of that book, that those who dwelt in darkness encountered the marvelous light. We've come to understand that interpretively speaking the great light was Jesus.  Ironically, those people although exposed to the great light of Jesus Christ, they never truly comprehended him.  They never really understood his purpose and his place in the grand scheme of their salvation.  They sought salvation.  They sought order, and they sought control over their lives but they sought it according to the system of the world in which they were now fully immersed.  They could only comprehend violent overthrow or insurgency.  They only understood deadly coup d'etats that would uproot the governmental system.  They could not understand the idea of divine revolution through submission to a holy God.

The New Testament nation of Israel living as a Roman-occupied colony generations removed from God's instruction and intervention in their lives, had diminished the experience of God to the ritualistic practice of temple sacrifice, and yearly sacramental feast.  God was boxed into a dwelling place behind the veil of their brocaded temples.  He spoke only from the pages of a well-worn Torah and only on the Sabbath.  He exercised only judgment through his long robed religiously attired scribes, and priest.  The fact was that Israel had spiritually betrayed the covenant they had made with God and had voluntarily reshackled themselves into an Egyptian-like enslavement.  Idolatry had been exchanged for religious excess and pandering, both lacked truth and spiritual substance.

American society today bears a history that mirrors the errors of ancient Israel.  A country founded essentially on the ideals of an orthodox Christian worldview has so strayed away from these roots that the wings upon which our eagles now fly are no more magnificent in expanse than the flightless wings of domesticated poultry; unable to get us off the ground level of existence much less soar.  As New Testament

# The Dusk of Mankind and the Dawn of the Kingdom

Israel teetered on the brink of extinction with full indistinguishable immersion into the Roman empire so too does America falter on the edge of losing its Christian character and identity for an atheistic, narcissistic and agnostic pale image of its former self. Fortunately, however, America like Israel has a powerful secret that upholds even the most tried faith. That secret is that the light of hope of the gospel of the kingdom is about to break forth in these last and evil days. As Israel seemed to be slowly disappearing under the foot of Roman tyranny, a great proclamation was made in the fields just outside the city of Bethlehem by angels to a group of lowly shepherds- who would become known as the first witnesses to the arrival of God's kingdom dominion on the earth. The angel's said while standing in darkness, "Unto us this day is born in the city of David, a savior who is Christ the Lord!" Oil was added to the flickering light of spiritual hope. My friend that same proclamation is being made, and oil is being released in this great nation. This nation, that appears to be slowly disappearing under the heel of consumerism, God abandonment, psychological terrorism; and the idolatry of fame and fortune is about to see the power of God released in such a way if the people of God would take up the mandate of kingdom reestablishment in the earth. God's kingdom is being birthed into the hearts, minds and spirits of men and women who are available for his using in fulfilling his purpose in this world.

To every factual fracture of the landscape of American society there is a real spiritual remedy tied to the ideology of God's kingdom influence in this world. Divorce, debt, disease and dysfunction that have become natural parts of the social order of our time are dilemmas that truly are vulnerable to a kingdom agenda. If and when we let God's kingdom come into our lives we force setbacks to the outskirts of our existence. Trouble, trials and tribulation are necessary character enforcing scenarios for a faith-led citizen of the kingdom. Jesus warned that trouble in this life, this world and this time was as expected as breathing was, to our very survival.

There is recovery after divorce. It is an unfortunate fact of contemporary life that divorce is a real fear of many marriages. It occurs readily and can leave scars of abandonment not only in the adults but also for the children involved. However, there is hope beyond divorce court. God does not endorse the practice but he does give room for pardon. God also can even use your experience of divorce to exact a good outcome in your life. The Bible says that all things work for the good of them that love the Lord and are called according to His purpose. People who divorce are not excluded from this group of people who love God. They too can earn a good reward for their love of God even after going through the "things" of divorce.

The disastrous statistics on divorce paints a picture of the apparent failure of the institution of marriage. The fight for the family being fought today by many faith-based organizations is commendable and may eventually bear the fruit of the successful rebirthing of traditional two-parent families. However, the approach of eviscerating those who have gone through broken relationships and taken the step to divorce will probably cause no greater reconciliation. But rather may lead to outright rejection of a central tenet of the Christian faith. For generations, men and women have committed spiritual suicide, walked away from church and from God because they felt unable to face the eyes, voices and critical analysis of the people of faith. My objective here is not to endorse turning a

# The Dusk of Mankind and the Dawn of the Kingdom

"blind eye" on acts of infidelity, and sin but we must not only call our fellow man to task; we must also help him or her to reestablish a forthright relationship foremost with God and then with those who've been affected by their decision.  Too often, we as Christians, air wholeheartedly on the side of retribution with little recourse on the side of restoration.  Someone's decision to have an affair is an act of sin but it is not an act of eternal separation from God.  Many times those who have affairs are not necessarily against marriage; in fact they seldom are.  They, in fact, have just gotten themselves into a place where they have lost sight of their moral compass and have allowed temptation to have the best of them.  God hates sin but most of all He loves us.  He hates when we do wrong but he relishes the moments and the occasions when we do right and repent.  Why do you think God dealt with ancient Israel as He did?  He could have cut them off, and started all over again with a new group of people but He chose to give them countless chances to come back to Him.  It is no wonder that God referred to Israel and eventually His chosen people, through His prophets, as a wayward bride, even a harlot who had betrayed the betrothal agreement many times but for whom He would grant a pardon.  God could have given up hope that mankind would ever get it right and created a whole new species.  However, in His infinite wisdom He created systems and ways by which even a fallen people could approach Him and experience His miraculous power.  He taught them systems of worship and sacrificial ritual that was to be the prototype of what true communion with Him would take.  God did this all with the intent of drawing us back to Him.  A great gulf had been created between us, partly because of our own selfish pursuits and partly because the enemy of our souls was determined to cut the umbilical cord of human connection to their creator.  But the devil's plot could never overthrow the

Creator's plan.  Plots are afterthoughts while plans are forethoughts.  The Bible says that God foreknew us.  He knew our uprisings and our down falling.  He did not want us to fall but He understood that failure was definitely a possibility as long as we walked dependent upon ourselves.  Divorce happens when we start to depend on ourselves to make two imperfect and uncomplimentary individuals a perfect union.  Our union in marriage depends on each individual getting in God first.  A vertical union must take place first before our horizontal unions have any hope of flourishing.  We may make mistakes in marriage.  We may even make mistakes in who we enter into marriage with, but after the dissolution, and after the realization we must ask ourselves if our mistake was due to us individually being out of alignment with God, or if the misalignment was in the decision.  There's one thing for a decision to be out of alignment but if *we* are out of alignment, no matter how many good decisions we make we will never be able to bear the relevant fruit of our sowing.

Think of it this way; an apple tree planted in the shade, watered daily, trimmed and whose soil is aerated on a regular basis may appear to be getting the best treatment.  Watering is good, trimming is good, and loosening the soil for the free flow of air is good but if the tree gets no sunlight it still won't bear the necessary fruit.  Apples may grow from that tree but they will lack the nutrients necessary for consumption.  Many marriages and other endeavors that we undertake can be made analogous to that of the experience of the young apple tree in the shade.  We may be doing all the right things to nurture the relationship and to be the husband that God would have us to be and the wife that God would have us to be.  However, if we were not first the man that God was calling for us to be, or the woman that God was calling you to be, or the mate that we chose was also not operating in godliness, our efforts to nurture a weak marriage would be futile.

There are scores of scarred men who don't attend church and even more women who sit in the latter pews of our sanctuaries privately ashamed of what they've done but reluctant to stay completely disconnected from God. There's the harsh reality of scorned ex-wives and reputation-riddled ex-husbands who are convinced that they have diminished their hopes of salvation because of divorce. The Bible speaks clearly on the issue in a few places but it speaks even more about God's faithfulness to forgive. As kingdom citizens we have a right to a royal pardon, and we have no right to hold the feet of others to the fire for an act of transgression. One of the greatest hindrances to the advancement of the kingdom mindset in a person's life is the obstacle of unforgiveness. Unforgiveness, in any form and for any reason is a prison. It is a prison that you, the one who harbors the unforgiveness, have the unenviable task and duty of being the doorkeeper. When you hold others in unforgiveness you place yourself in a prison of experience and you limit your ability to interact, pursue and get involved in the activities of life. Unforgiveness causes us to avoid certain places, people and situations stifling our chances to experience a fulfilled life, because we want to somehow make this other person feel hurt through our rejection of them. However, tragically, the subject of our unforgiveness metastasizes from a subject to an object. Unforgiveness causes this personal grudge to materialize from being a personal situation to a divisive and invasive condition that rules our life. The subject of our derision is seldom aware of the uneasiness that they present to our lives. Sometimes even if they had been aware at one time they soon forget. This leaves us as the agents of our own misery constantly reviving in our own souls memories of hurt, and tarnished feelings-memories the other person had long left in some storehouse of their past.

    Retrieve the key to your prison, and let yourself out. Let yourself go and pray for that person who hurt you. Pray to God for the will to love them the way he loves us. Pray to God like Jesus prayed to God to forgive them for they know not what they did. Release yourself and others from the shackles of legalism that you yourself are unable to bear. And thank God for the grace to see past the pain they caused you. Thank God for what you learned, not about them, but about yourself in the process. Let the hurt be a lesson in learning more about you.

## Kingdom Keys *on Facing the Facts about Family*

    The institution of the family is a foundational component of kingdom life. It was God that said in the book of Genesis, in the second chapter account of creation, "It is not good that man should be alone." It was upon the conclusion of this declaration that God determined parenthetically that man needed help. He needed assistance in the meeting of his needs before God. God loves us individually and expects us to have a personal relationship with Him. But he also recognizes that we need people of our own kind who can fulfill our natural needs for companionship. In Adams relationship with God, Adam was given clear direction and received spiritual impartation to not only rule but also to protect. However, that relationship as wonderful and spiritually fulfilling as it was, lacked the necessary ingredient to make the physical component of man satisfied and yet still achieve the mandate to be fruitful and multiply. God is enough company for us spiritually, but physically He is unable to condescend to

# The Dusk of Mankind and the Dawn of the Kingdom

fulfill us naturally. This is where family comes in. Family is designed to fill in the gap when a sense of loneliness may engulf us.

Why is family a necessary part of the kingdom? Family is the foundation, location and the vertical dimension within which God will ordain his blessing. Family is the place where your identity is forged, and fortified. It is the soil within which your seed is kept, nurtured and given the life necessary for complete germination. Family is the bedrock in which God translates kingdom order, and educates mankind about the sequence of divine succession. In the family, the man is the head and stands as a representative image of God's headship over the entire world. Your family is your world. The woman, embodied in the wife, represents the bride. Spiritually speaking the bride is symbolic of the church and if the church is the bride that means that she is to be a helpmate to her groom who is Christ. The church that is deeply entrenched in fulfilling the kingdom agenda must understand its responsibility in assisting God in the implementation of His kingdom governing principles in the earth. The church is in turn charged with the duty of upholding the tenets of marriage and traditional family values in this society. The family in the traditional sense is to be a microcosm of the kingdom.

Men are given power and authority to manage the interests of heaven's kingdom in the earth. They are called to be faithful stewards, walk justly, love mercy and execute God's will and purpose in the earth realm. This should be done with an air of humility. Our humility is vested in the fact that it is not by our might, power or strength that we possess what we have, and are able to do what we can but it is by God's spirit. Man's authority must be guided by the executive influence of God's spirit, then and only then will the family regain its significance as something to be pursued in contemporary society.

Kingdom Strategies *for the Family*
-Lead the family in prayer regularly.

-Devote time to daily reading and study of God's Word (familiarizing yourself with His will)

-Invest in the kingdom-the best investment is always that which has the greater return. Consider all that God does for us with little investment on our part. Now imagine if you sowed into God's divine purpose. The harvest would be incalculable.

-Get involved in kingdom work. Do something in the kingdom that sincerely makes a difference without seeking a reward. Use your skills, talents and gifts without a thought for repayment but with a heart for positively impacting others, easing someone's burden, and making life that much more agreeable for someone less fortunate.
-Join a Bible believing church that practices what it preaches. One that has leadership that has a vision closely tied to the vision of Jesus for His people in His kingdom. Help a godly man or woman advance their God given vision.

-But most of all, be an example of godliness first in your family, then in your community. Love God in such a way that your children will take notice and develop a love for Him as well. Provide, protect and guide your family in a path that patterns how God provides, protects and guides you.

# The Dusk of Mankind and the Dawn of the Kingdom

## Chapter Two

## Overcoming the giant named, FEAR

Many of us can look resolutely back at our lives and recall episodes, occasions and even seasons of our life when we were frustrated by fear.  For some of us fear created indecision; and now as we stand several years removed from being frozen by fear in that decision, we now realize that there are so many things that we should've accomplished already but we were not able to because of the hindrance of fear.  A host of us are returning to the classroom as adults because as young men and women fear of underachieving or simply of being unable to afford a higher education kept us out of even considering college.  Others of us allowed fear to box us into a job or a career that was and still is way below our potential.  Fear of being ill prepared to function at a higher level kept us stagnant.  Fear held another group of us into holding patterns of unfulfilling personal relationships.  Due to the onset of fear many of us stayed and dealt with abuse, both physically and mentally. It was a fear that we could not do any better, a fear that made us take the lumps and swallow many bitter pills just so that we could escape loneliness, while still pushing ourselves deeper into it.

Fear is a powerful force. It is a force so powerful that it could paralyze our progress, stifle our success and cause us to die prematurely. Fear garners its power from the same realm as faith. Although fear is a cheap imitation of faith it is one that can create comparative results. Fear depends on ones innermost weakness. It feeds on our darkest expectations and therefore is fueled by anxiety. To fear is to anticipate the worse. Fear works in its effort to make the unlikely real because when we walk in fear we create the circumstances for our own failure. All we have to do to make our fears come to pass is to stop moving, turn back or give up; sooner or later our fears will overtake us.

The Bible says that God has not given us a spirit of fear. That means that fear is a product of the devil. It is a fabrication of the kingdom principle of faith. Faith imagines a thing coming to pass while fear pictures it never coming to fruition. Faith is a realization of a former hope, and fear is an actualization of a present worry.

Fear is the uncompromising giant in the life of the believer. Ignorance ensnares the unbeliever but fear traps the believer. The only sure strategy to stop a believer with a promise spoken over their lives is to speak fear into their soul (i.e. their will). The devil can't stop God from blessing you but he can cause you to forsake your blessing in fear. God gave the children of Israel the Promised Land. He spoke a promise-a covenanted surety-into the life of Abraham, Isaac and Jacob. But yet still Joshua after leading the descendants of these great men of promise into the land still had to convince them that they had to actively possess it. The promise of God was not going to be passively transmitted to them. They still had to go in and aggressively take what God had said was theirs. This is a scenario that is ripe for fear to set in. All Israel had to do was to look at the circumstances before them. They were a band of desert wanderers encroaching on a fruitful land that they were told was theirs, but that was occupied by people who appeared to be established and powerful. The atmosphere was set for them to either walk in great faith, or for them to cower in great fear. And this is what the enemy desires to do in our lives. He desires for us to be faced with great challenges of our faith and for us to choose fear, and deny ourselves receipt of the promise.

Fear is a bedfellow of doubt and a hamper of promise. They are intimately related and depend on each other for sustenance. Every unfulfilled divine promise has its roots in the quagmire of fear and doubt. Doubt often is a great indicator of the presence of fear. The voice of doubt is always produced by the mind of fear. If you think fearfully, you'll speak doubtfully. The strength of the infamous Philistine giant, Goliath was vested in the ability of Goliath to strike fear in his enemies. His very presence in the camp of the Philistines imputed fear upon the Israelite army. King Saul and his forces stood frozen in fear and Goliath loomed larger with every word of doubt and every sigh of unbelief that emanated from the Israelite camp.

How many of you reading this book thus far can point to a time when your speech was driven by fear even before you tried? Shakespeare once said that our doubts are traitors, and makes us lose the good we oft might win by fearing to attempt. We lose out on much

## The Dusk of Mankind and the Dawn of the Kingdom

good when we fail to attempt a thing simply out of fear. We waste opportunities for greatness when we fear. What if Moses had continued to doubt his ability to be a deliverer for his people? What if he had continued to present excuses for why he wasn't adequately equipped? Most of our fears like Moses' are unfound. And what we usually fear about has already been taken care of by God but we miss it because we fearfully go the other way, or we disobey God and we stay right where we are. We continue to tend to someone else's flock on the backside of the desert and we settle for obscurity and mediocrity.

"I can't do it! I'm not qualified! No one in my family has ever done it! I don't know what it is to be a father! I'm not ready for marriage. I'm not good enough to give my life over to the Lord!" These comments are the fruit of doubt and fear. After facing the harsh facts of life our minds are triggered to fire these doubt laced comments into the atmosphere but it is a trick of the enemy. Opening our eyes to face the reality of a contradictory world can be the most daunting task we undertake in our salvation. It's the first picture we see after the cloud of exaltation over our salvation settles. But retreating in fear isn't the answer; instead we must go forth in faith. However, between the echo of doubt and the advance in faith there must be a decision made to believe. Belief must precede faith because if faith came first then it would be literally pseudo-faith. Pseudo-faith steps out hesitantly and hopes that it has ground to stand on. But real faith is being sure of what I hoped for (past tense) and certain of what I do not see in the present.

The giant of fear must die in our lives. Kingdom minded men and women understand that giants are no match for kingdom faith. Kingdom faith speaks to mountains and orders them to be uprooted and relocate, and they do it. How then can a mere giant expect to block you from your blessing? David killed his giant and it cleared the way to victory for an entire nation. The death of a giant in your life will not only create a release in your life but it will also free all of those connected to you, to go forth in the realization of their delayed destinies.

On a personal note when I killed the giant of fear in my life, I was able to push the dreams of those that depended on me to a place of realization. If I had not gotten over my hang-ups about marriage my wife might probably have never achieved some of the things that she has been able to accomplish. Simply because of my yes, and my refusal to allow fear to overrun my life she was able to go back to school, take a summer off of work and earn her Master's degree, while I stayed working and taking care of home. Defeating fear allowed us to make the sacrifice of moving from renting a three-room studio style apartment that was financially within our reach to making the sacrifice and stepping out to purchase a two-family house that seemed economically out of our reach. If I'd never overcome the fear of failure I would not be in the process of writing yet another book, and opening additional streams of income to support and sustain my family. Fear always works against what's best for us. Fear is a false prophet always predicting failure and reminding us of our shortcomings.

The great battle of the ages in the human consciousness is that which is designed to control our inward fears and impute upon them outward faith. We war in the spirit because on the inside fear has taken up residence. Then we are trying to conjure up faith from the outside to overcome the damage that fear has

## The Dusk of Mankind and the Dawn of the Kingdom

done. In many of us there is this civil war already raging but unfortunately it is being controlled by our flesh and not by our spirits. The flesh is cleaving to fear and the spirit is clinging to courage in faith but that faith is lacking in force.

The Bible says that God has not given us a spirit of fear but of love, peace and a sound mind. That leaves us to ask if God hasn't given us fear well who has? We have to understand that the very thing that so easily besets us is that which comes from a source that is out to destroy us. Fear is like a weed growing in the midst of a field of grass. Like grass the weed needs very little tending or gardening care in order to reproduce. Whatever, little water that is applied to it during the paltry rainy season is enough for it to rear its ugly head. Fear needs little urging to reproduce. All it needs is a suggestion. A hint of failure or weakness is all that fear needs to reproduce and grow in strength and choke out all the faith that we do possess.

Fear prepares the human mind for a perceived pending predicament. But unfortunately, it is preparation that is predicated on false information. It is a preparation that is based in assumption. And the devil knows that his best bet is to get you into the clutch of fear. Because it is in fearing that we will surrender hope. It is in fear that we will settle for good and forsake great. It is in fear that we will give up climbing at the doorsill of our deliverance. Fear is the great equalizer of forward thinking people. It hinders progress and punctuates victory.

As long as I court fear I will be reluctant to seek a better job, or better relationships, or a greater prayer life. Fear brings my forward motion to a grinding halt. It is the devil's greatest apparatus next to outright deception.  If I cannot outright deceive you, I sure can cause you to fear the unknown.

Fallen human nature is predisposed to irrational fear.  This is because sin has caused a disconnect that overrules the trust that once existed between God and man.  God trusted Adam with his entire creation and we know this because God told him to name it, rule over it or have dominion.  Giving man dominion means to give man authority.  There is authority even in being given the duty of naming a thing.  The process of determining nomenclature is an act of imputing ownership upon a thing.  When God gave man the authority to name as well as to rule we got a picture of perfect trust.  You were given the right to name and the right to rule, that which wasn't even yours to begin with.

But sin created a separation.  Sin came in and corrupted what God had established as pure.  But God is faithful and just, and he would not have us to be eternally separated.  He desires reconciliation but He does understand that it will require sacrifice, and what greater sacrifice than having to give up what is most precious to us in order that another might be saved.  As I have closely studied fear and its relationship to faith over the years I have come to the conclusion that fear is as a result of the human natures inclination to independence while still being aware of its imperfections and inabilities.  Human nature strives to seek independent existence but is reminded when brought to a moment of weakness that it still needs to stay connected to a source that is greater than itself.

One of the reoccurring failures of the faith has been that of forsaking self for the benefit of others.  It is easy to forsake the world, and it is easy to forsake sin but it is doubly difficult to forsake self.  To forsake self

# The Dusk of Mankind and the Dawn of the Kingdom

is to put others ahead of us. The problem with it is that human nature finds it hard to condescend to its own selfishness. The flesh feeds on that which satisfies it, even if just for a little while. To forsake self is to assume a posture of humility. We are fearful of humility because we equate it with humiliation. We believe that if we were to humble ourselves under the mighty hand of God that we would be soon humiliated by men.

Fear keeps us in a mindset of self-preservation. Everything that we do falls along the lines of that which benefits us or that which shields us from exposure to harmful actions, thoughts and attachments. We cringe at the thought of sacrifice because we understand that it takes giving up something.

Jacob feared the possibility of encountering a vengeful Esau. How many of you have lived most of your early adult life in fear of crossing paths with those whom you've hurt in your past? How many of you have no problem speaking about them, thinking about them, respecting them from a distance, but find it impossible to come face to face with them? Jacob's fear was based on real evidence. He did deceive Esau, he did steal his blessing, he did trick him out of a birthright. He did co-opt his blessing and Godly favor. But it was still a fear grounded in his human condition. He had prayed to God. He had gotten revelation from God, and God had spoken promise not of future things but of present favor and yet still the ghost of his past whispered defeat. He's coming with 400 men, four hundred warring men, and four hundred angry men. These were real fears based on unreal assumptions.

The fears are real from a human perspective but unreal from a Godly perspective. If God said it, and placed a guarantee upon it by His Word, then it shall come to pass and there's nothing the devil could do about it. God's Word is as good as a Godly guarantee. It is an unlimited warranty not limited by time, space or money.

Jacob believed God because he saw God do it for him in the past. God prospered him, gave him great increase in family and possessions but yet still fear of his past caused him to fall into doubt. Why would God bring you out with more than you went in with only to leave you to be destroyed?

Some of us believe God for things but we doubt God when it comes to restoring our relationships. We believe Him for wealth but we doubt that He is able to forgive us. These are all rooted in the giant of fear. God never does an incomplete work. He finishes what he starts. He shall cause it to come to pass and nothing that you have been through, experienced or been exposed to was for nothing. It was meant to bring you into maturity from fearful living to faithful living; from doubt to hope; from war to peace; from sadness to joy; from unbelief to belief; from insecurity to trust. As we enter into the holy place of God's everlasting presence in our lives we are made vulnerable to the impact of God's glory and power in our lives. And even then we can and may be consumed with fear like the Israelites were when God came down like a fiery cloud on Mt. Sinai in the wilderness sojourn of his promised people. But it is in that fear that we ascend to wisdom. Proverbs teaches us that the fear of God is the beginning of wisdom. That is the only fear that we should pursue; a healthy fear of God, and a fearlessness for the shadows of this world.

# The Dusk of Mankind and the Dawn of the Kingdom

Kingdom Keys **on *Fear***

The fear of the extinction of the role of fathers in our society is a direct result of the demonic influence on the kingdom of this world targeted at dismantling the symbolic representation of God in the family. Fatherhood has unfortunately become an option for many men in our society. Why do I consider it unfortunate? It's unfortunate because fatherhood should be the rule and not an option. However, the sharply rising percentage of unwed, single or separated mothers raising children on their own is pointing to that fact. A large portion of men have undoubtedly chosen to forego the responsibility of playing a part in the raising of children that they played a part in conceiving. I would be remissed not to mention the young men out there who've attempted to play an integral role but were denied that privilege either by the judicial system or by a scorned woman. Nevertheless, the numbers of those who have skirted their responsibility and continue to skirt it far outnumbers those who endure the lengthy legal process or the raking of their reputation through the coals by a rejected female.

Yes, it is difficult trying to "stake your claim" as an estranged father. It is no secret that our legal system shows marked favoritism toward mothers in issues of custody and support. The motherly instinct is given precedence but that doesn't mean fathers are unnecessary. Society, courts, and any number of popular talk show hosts may espouse the doctrine of the empowered independent single mother. However, that does not deem the practice a sanctioned arrangement, at least not divinely. Just ask any number of children raised or being raised in a single parent home. Interview the average young mother raising an adolescent or pre-pubescent boy alone and the responses that you hear would be generally the same. "I'm getting along fine but", is how it begins. There's always a but. There's the, but I don't know how to handle his moods. Or the, but sometimes he just always asks about his father who I hardly hear from. Or the, but he doesn't seem to appreciate all that I'm doing for him, he still says that he wished that he was living with his "good-for-nothing" father. Or the, but he's getting too big for me to handle.

The stories are the same and the responses are harsh. I have the privilege of being on the frontline of such parental worries working for the past ten years in the field of public education in an urban setting. It never fails to happen that the majority of young men labeled as behavioral problems are the products of fatherless homes-either literally or figuratively. Fatherlessness is disputably the number one cause of social maladjustment in the adolescent and teen years for both boys and girls. This trend is further exacerbated by the virtual extinction of male educators, and other such male role models within the context of their early nurturing. Both boys and girls need to see positive images of men. They need to have the experience of interaction, counsel and correction from a man. It leaves an indelible mark that can virtually lay the foundation for how they consider an almighty father in heaven. Boys learn how to be men from their exposure to real men. Girls learn how a woman should be treated and respected by the way the men in their lives treat and respect the women around them.

I understand personally the effect and impact that a father has on a young man's identity and character. I have been in both situations as an outsider looking in at the young men that I interact with each year. Then as an insider looking out at how I had to deal with the disappointment of a less than present father.  The epidemic of fear that exists among men today about assuming the role of fatherhood is an area or condition that must be dealt with immediately if we are to make any inroads on the negative trends facing the next generation of young people in our society.  As W.E.B DuBois said, "Men must not only know, they must do!"  They must not only know what detriment their absence is causing but they must take steps to stem the tide, and the inevitable backlash that will follow if nothing is ever done to address it.

Where do we begin to overcome the fear of fatherhood?  First, we must demystify the whole experience.  Fatherhood does not require experts or perfectionist, just a willing and sincere heart.  Hearing of the significance of fathers, to the lives of their sons and daughters may be intimidating, especially when you consider personal examples of when it was lacking in your own life.  A few generations ago the issue wasn't absent fathers.  It was present fathers who existed as silent partners in the rearing of their children.  The problem which wasn't seen as a problem at the time was that although the family was intact-the image of the breadwinning, workaholic strong, silent-type father created a generation of men who expected women to handle the kids and the home, just as long as they brought home the bread.  This expectation went contrary to another developing trend, that of the women's liberation movement.  While men were being patterned into one way of thinking about the dynamic of the family, women were being taught the concepts of self-empowerment, freedom from the entrapments of the fundamentalist child-rearing philosophy and told that they did not have to settle for being homemakers any longer.

You could imagine the resistance and the backlash that these trends created for each other. Men were expected to adjust to liberated, career-seeking women, and women were in turn expected to cope with men with little sense of their important role in the active rearing of children.

As a father of two children, one with whom I live, and the other who lives with her mother's relatives, I have to deal with a mixed bag of feelings as well. There are times when I feel that I should be doing more to make my older daughter a more integral part of my immediate life. However, in my zeal to fulfill some personal perception of being a mentally deadbeat dad, I often realize that for me to pull my daughter out of the dynamic of living with her grandparents and cousins would be more about satisfying my own ego than doing her any ultimate good. As a result I just make sure that I do the essential things, like maintain my financial support and keep the lines of communication open, and make sacrifices to put funds aside to either visit her or have her visit us. This is done all while trying to maintain a cordial relationship with the parents who do have daily contact with her. My arrangement is not the ideal, or the perfect one but it is the most adequate for all the parties involved. I could never discourage a fellow father from doing his utmost legally to get in contact with a child that the mother is barring him from seeing. However, I would encourage those fathers to keep all options open and to never allow anger to be the dictate of how they pursue legal ends. Anger like fear never works for us it always cogitates against what's beneficial.

Kingdom Strategies *for Fathers*
-Accept your responsibility for bearing children.

# The Dusk of Mankind and the Dawn of the Kingdom

-Start small: - Do little things to become a greater part of your child's life. Designate unrehearsed occasions when you read to your son or daughter.

-Make arrangements even if occasionally to drop off or pick up your child from school. Establish consistency even if it is once a week or once a month. Your consistency shows care and concern.

-Open lines of communication: - Speak to your children not only about the facts of life but more so about your life. Let them see that you struggle, and that you too have fears.

-Build a heritage for your offspring. Invest your finances in such a way that you have some money to spare.

-Build a Christian based spiritual heritage where you show the example of a prayerful life, biblical study, persistent devotion regardless of challenges and Godly purpose.

Hugh J. Harmon

# The Dusk of Mankind and the Dawn of the Kingdom

## Chapter Three

### Running on Empty

*And the angel of the Lord came again the second time, and touched him, and said, Arise and eat: because the journey is too great for thee.*

1 Kings 19:7

With record high gas prices almost assaulting us daily, it isn't surprising that we may from time to time encounter the red flashing signal in our cars silently screaming at us, "Check the gauge!" Just about every car that is up to the muster when it comes to inspections is able to warn its driver that it's literally running on empty. It is then that some of us frantically scan the horizon for the looming sign of a service station. Some drivers even lose their cool and swerve in and out of traffic in exuberance just to slide their vehicle into a gas station with its entrance three lanes to the right in bumper-to-bumper traffic. While driving with a flashing "Check the gauge" light we get

## The Dusk of Mankind and the Dawn of the Kingdom

desperate. Our desperation is based on the fear of being stuck.

After facing the facts of our human condition, and subsequently killing the giant of fear that frustrates us, many times we find ourselves operating on empty. We're empty because we're in a place where we realize that our sum abilities and skills are not enough to make life work for us. The common concern of mankind, rich or poor is the issue of making life work for them. Making life work can be defined as the task of negotiating the peaks and pitfalls of life's experiences while still maintaining the initiative to press on. When we come to a place where we no longer desire moving on, the only other option is death. Unfortunately, fallen human nature has a propensity toward choosing death.

Why does humanity choose death more often than life? The unpredictability of life, and the prevalence of trouble regardless of social status, wealth or even religious persuasion make the permanent decision of death for the temporary inconvenience of trouble most inviting. It is because death, when running on empty is always a more inviting option. The flesh does not relish death but if put into a tight place it will choose death over life especially when life is a challenge. It will choose death because death is a quick fix for pain.

Mankind will never correctly pursue the things of life because in order to do that he must adopt a spirit of faith. In order for us to live abundantly in a world that by its very nature cogitates against me attaining any level of comfort, I've got to assume a posture of faith. Adopting a faith perspective allows us the leeway to see troubling circumstances, hear negative forecasts, and even encounter setbacks while still resting in an internal assurance that everything will work out for my good.  A faith perspective says that where I am right now hurts and it doesn't feel good to my flesh but it is good for my soul.  Jesus said, "In this world you shall have trouble."  The fact that Jesus said you shall means that trouble is literally an obligation or a promise that we have to endure.  However, it does not mean that it is indefensible.  You shall means that trouble is a conditional outgrowth of life in this fallen world.  If you're alive, you're going to encounter it, but if you live by faith your experience of trouble will not be considered a directive to die.

As the kingdom of God endeavors to be made manifest in the earthly realm through the activity of the Holy Spirit, deposits of faith are being made available to people.  We have to understand that for faith to take root, the ground into which it must be planted has to be cleared for cultivation.  Before vegetable or fruit farmers sow seeds into a parcel of land they must first cultivate that parcel of land.  They must prepare the land through fostering it for the task of growing something tangible.  Cultivation not only prepares the land to bear a harvest but the act of clearing and tilling the land improves its ability to produce or to give birth to a great crop.  Cultivation refines the land.  It institutes a growth culture into that parcel of land.  The Spirit of God, the chief agent of kingdom acculturation works in us after salvation to cultivate the thorny fields of our hearts, souls and spirits.

Salvation causes us to face the facts of our faulty life, and God's grace when granted gives us the power to overcome our fears.  The renewal and the regeneration that salvation brings, puts us in a position of vulnerability because we no longer walk by our strength or by our will but by His will.

# The Dusk of Mankind and the Dawn of the Kingdom

When I am running on empty in salvation, with expectancy of God's deliverance; despite how weak I feel, and how inept I consider myself, I know that I'm in the best place possible. Salvation wipes our slate clean; it filters out the filth from my engine and sets me up to receive the oil of God's anointing, appointing and engaging power. If I never get emptied out I'm liable to have an episode of spontaneous combustion because my soulish man still tied to worldly concerns would not be able to handle the influx of God's power. The Bible asks how can two walk together unless they be agreed. Additionally, it says that there is no fellowship between darkness and light. Part of you can't want God, and the other parts want the world and that arrangement work out! One of your parts will eventually consume the other. The medical disorder known as pulmonary tuberculosis is often termed in colloquial terms as "consumption". It is called consumption because it is a literal wasting away of body tissue beginning in the lungs. This is all due to a constriction of pulmonary vessels that are deprived of oxygen by the build-up of fluid in the lungs. Many of us are suffering from spiritual consumption. Our spirit man is being deprived of the life preserving and sustaining oxygen of the breath of God's Spirit-the *ruach* of God. Therefore, our souls, spirits and even our flesh are wasting away in sin, sexual perversion, immoral thinking, waste, greed and excess. We are drowning internally on bacteria-infested fluids. But if we turn by repenting; surrender whom we are and what we have, by way of not only our possessions but also our personality, even that which is contrary to Him, and we ask the kingdom of God to set up residence within us then we can initiate our emptying in His presence.

How do you know when you need to be emptied?  It is at the times when you feel most helpless to stave off undesirable feelings.  It is when you find yourself in a relationship that looked good at the outset but now feels very different than you imagined.  You need emptying when you find yourself compromising more often than you find yourself complementing.  You need to be emptied when you're settling for harsh criticism more than you're receiving encouraging compliments.  Accepting a call to emptiness is never comfortable.  I don't believe there's record of any human being that has faced the ordeal of emptying without feeling a sense of the pain of withdrawal.  It's like dealing with illegal drugs, when you were an unsaved sinner you were literally addicted to sin and had an inclination to failure.  Before you heard the Word of faith that removed the block from your ears and gave you new hearing you were incapable of choosing otherwise.  Faith gives us more options to choose from.  It gives us the options of either choosing faith that would lead to success, or to choose to fear that would lead to failure.  Without faith, fear and death are the only options.  Faith is the proverbial way of escape that God promises in every instance of the onset of temptation.  It opens a door in a closed room with close quarters and the temptation being at arm's length.  Faith is my way of escape in the kingdom.

How is my emptying accomplished?  For many individuals who find themselves on the fence when it comes to believing in the efficacy and even the existence of salvation is the issue of them not accepting that it is something that is totally out of their hands.  Beyond being open-minded to receiving an invitation to know God in a personal way we really don't have the power to save ourselves.  Therefore, empowered, self-willed, self-actualized, and independent loving men and women find it difficult to grasp the idea of God choosing them, and not them choosing God. We love to believe that there is some trigger sparked by intellectual attainment or ironically intellectual decline that prompts the human mind to even want to have God in their lives. For centuries, Christians as with many other systems of religious belief have been criticized for lacking some intellectual quotient. This lack predisposed them to want to bow to a God that had all the answers to the many questions they had. Science the religion of acquiring worldly knowledge has convinced many individuals that humanity if given enough time will eventually be able to explain all things. However, if we accept the premise that the survival of humanity depends on the blue print, guide and manual that our manufacturer produced about us we will know that science is a drop in the bucket of the knowledge necessary to comprehend just who we are.

To accept that you need emptying is to understand that you are vessels that can be poured into as well as out of. The Bible refers to humanity as earthen vessels. That means that we are vessels made of dust and dirt, and fashioned with the purpose and intent of holding something valuable or precious.

*But we have this treasure in earthen vessels, that the excellency of the power may be of God and not of us.*
2 Corinthians 4:7

Even more deeply needed is the understanding that what we were, prior to salvation, corrupted vessels. We had lost the ability to carry God's anointing. Therefore in our rebirth God had to break us like spoiled pottery and cast us back into the refiner's fire so that we might be made fit to be formed into a new vessel.

*And the vessel that he made of clay was marred in the hand of the potter: so he made it again another vessel, as seemed good to the potter to make it.*
Jeremiah 18:4

The kingdom-minded believer must expect breaking to take place in their lives. This is because without breaking there is no release, no pouring out, no emptying and hence no room made for pouring of the oil of the spirit.

The first years of salvation are the most challenging for a believer because they're looking for all that God promised, to be instantaneously manifested in their lives. Most of us expected our debt relief to be immediate. We truly believed the preacher when he said expect to receive an unanticipated financial deposit into our bank account. And some of us were devastated when we didn't see it happen. We expected to go back to the doctor and hear that we were cured the Monday after we gave our life to the Lord. Some women thought that their husbands would miraculously turn around in his attitude and behavior concerning marriage and the family, but he didn't. It's at these times that God was pouring out of us all our expectations so as to make room for us to focus on his expectations.

The male species, probably find this aspect of salvation to be the most effacing of the male character. The idea of having to be emptied out is viewed by the male ego as condescension that borders on humiliation. To be emptied is to be weakened and put into a state of dependence upon others. Manhood has so long been distinguished by the idea of independence, and freedom

## The Dusk of Mankind and the Dawn of the Kingdom

of will that any level of emptying would naturally cogitate against accepted manly character. However, for women emptying is a spiritual offshoot of the natural emptying that accompanies an adult female's monthly cycle. Women are better emotionally equipped to deal with the feeling of dependence on others than are men. Women are raised in our society many times with a greater sense of responsibility in the execution of family duties. While men are simply shown love and are expected to fall into the groove of providing for and protecting their family. Dependence is inculcated into the feminine psyche and independence and self-determination is engrained in the male psyche.

Regardless of the ease or the disease with which females and males respectively cope with God's emptying, it is an experience that they have to deal with. The issue then shifts from whether emptying is necessary or real, but rather we must consider what shall we do after the emptying. What must we endeavor to do in the aftermath of our breaking and pouring out? How do we live beyond the reconciliation and reckoning of that which was in us that had to be removed? How do we live with the knowledge of the ugliness that once was us? How do we go on, knowing that we were the perpetrators of emotional damage done unto others? How do we recover after realizing that our setbacks were self-inflicted? How do we face the fact that all that we've become is as a result of our diminutive thinking, destructive self-image and poor self-esteem? God doesn't just clean us out He also allows us to see what He took out of us. We have to understand that emptying is not a secret experience. He doesn't take it out of us in our sleep, because we'll never know what was wrong with us if God took it secretly. There's got to be a confrontation that takes place. God turns our heads toward our mess, and our minds toward our crimes so that we might accept guilt.  It's not a confrontation created for you to engage in conflict but rather it is designed to give you a look at all that God is delivering and had delivered you from.  You should never tell anyone else that God has never done anything for you.  Just to be allowed life even though I was such a troublemaker, and a rabble-rouser.  God was faithful to you even though you were dwelling in faithlessness.

If we take a sheet out of the Samaritan woman's story we'll get an idea of how you should live after the emptying.  She came to the well to take a drink but ended up being emptied by Jesus.  The essence of it is that after she was emptied God immediately filled her through the Word spoken by Jesus.  She came face-to-face with who she was and whose she was and she was made whole.  Her emptying and her filling happened coincidentally and simultaneously.

As a former track and field, and cross-country athlete, I would like to borrow from the runner's vocabulary to further define this principle.  Any fellow runners would understand the following analogy.  There is a place in Jesus, like there's a place in distance running when our body's get into a groove that is uncomfortable.  It's a place where you feel that you've given your all, and all that you could do is put one foot before the other in a running action.  You have your head down and the terrain appears not to change despite every progressive stride you take.  You've given it all and it feels like the finish line will never come.  The only thing keeping you going isn't even your will; it's really the propensity of the muscles in your legs to press forward because they have been moving forward with purpose for so long already.

It's the same with the spirit, all it needs is an injection of purpose and a goal, and despite the physical pain, it will go forth undeterred.  Many times in long distance races, runners hit a zone where the body continues to run forward, but the mind becomes disengaged and hits a wall.  For any observer of track and field competition one can immediately identify when an athlete has hit that barrier where the memory inculcated in the limbs, ligaments and tendons from months of training keeps him or her going forward despite the fact that their countenance looks defeated.

When you're running on empty with God there's a disconnection created between the mind, which is our will, and our flesh.  When we're running on empty with God we're running a race that our minds can't comprehend, and our bodies find difficult to complete- but it's a race with a reward called God's Spirit.

The only reason some of us are even able to continue in the race is not because we have the skills and talents necessary to conquer the character of the disconnection.  But rather, we are able to continue because we can see the finish line.  We can see past the illogical conclusions, and the incomprehensible pain of the separation of our souls from our spirits; and we can see God's Spirit taking up residence on the inside.

The idea and the experience of running on empty is one that some of us come to through our new birth experience.  Others of us come to our point of emptiness as a result of poor life choices.  In these instances our emptiness came due to physical or mental abuse that was experienced over an extended period of time.  It was a forced emptying that caused more damage to us than was expected.

Life for many men and women in and outside of the body of Christ, unfortunately, can be described as life running on empty. Our lives become episodes of weathering storm after storm and just thanking God that we were able to hold on and survive. Our foundation scripture becomes, *"when the enemy came in like a flood, God lifted up a standard against him"* and we survived. It's good to depend on God in times of trouble and to recognize His hand in your daily deliverance but we must move from the place of daily being one step away from disaster. The abundant life that God determined to send His son to secure for us should not be a life that is about just keeping our heads above the water. It should be a life of conquering obstacles and supernaturally overcoming, time and time again.

The men and women that are caught in this vicious cycle of unfulfilled living, find themselves in one of two categories; the perpetrators of abuse or the victims of abuse. The truly dangerous aspect of abuse is the fact that it is injurious to both parties involved. It destroys the person receiving the abuse by taking from their self-esteem and defiles the person being the abuser by attaching to him or her, a spirit of anger and entitlement that transforms their lives too. There are no winners when it comes to abuse. The victim is obviously deeply scarred both on the outside and the inside, and the man or woman inflicting the abuse often unwittingly become pawns in a treacherous game of demonic control.

How many abusers have reported that they simply could not control their anger? Sometimes not only the victim feels trapped by the circumstances but also we find abusers who would describe their inability to stay "below the line" in their outward emotions as some kind of emotional snare.

Abuse regardless of its form and regardless of who is affected is a despicable consequence of a world out of control. Young kids are running on empty in our communities afraid of going home because of the mental brow beating or the physical manhandling that they will receive at the hands of an irate, ill-prepared parent. Women are running on empty facing daunting problems all due to the effects of abuse. We have women bruised and bearing scars of an insecure mate. We also have women facing the decision of whether to go through with a pregnancy for a man that has been nothing but harm to her peace and safety. There are women thrown out on the streets and made homeless by the men who no longer find anything in them worth pursuing. Statistics indicate that women far outnumber men in the status of being abused. I personally believe that the distinction is less than it appears, and although the incidences of men being abused may never equate to that of women, the problem is equally detrimental to both groups.

## *Kingdom Keys* **on Running on Empty in Abuse**

What can you do if your predicament is one of forced emptying as a result of abuse? What do you tell someone who has surrendered their self-esteem and settled for abuse because it seems more safe than loneliness? How do you minister to a victim that does not believe that they could ever trust again? We've got to give them someone to trust and something to hope in. We've got to not only rationally offer hope by how we talk in opposition to abuse, but we must make that opposition evident in our actions. Let them know that they are better than someone's punching bag.

Maybe you are the one that's been abused. We've got to understand that every negative experience, if we live to see it pass away, is merely part of our transition to the next level of living or the second part of our life. With that mindset we will realize that there's life on the other side of hurt and disappointment. Not every man will treat you the way he did. Not every woman will try to take advantage of you the way she did. We've all got to understand that the devil is determined to hinder us at all cost. He'll use any means necessary to turn us away from the path of righteousness. What better way to turn us, than to so stigmatize us concerning abuse that we decide to consider it a part of life and in some cases a normal one?

Abuse is a cancer that was demonically loosed into this world. It was designed to slowly erode the foundation of marriage, parenthood and family. Scores of battered women are finding their way to shelters throughout this land to escape abuse. However, in turn they are forced to make the difficult choice of their own safety, security and sanity over the duty of providing for family. Hence, even more scores of children are being left, and become eventual wards of the state because an abused mother had to escape, and an abusive father was incapable of providing the proper nurturing needed for developing children.

The children of abuse make up a large percentage of those who choose to live precariously on the streets. These children both male and female end up engaging in life threatening, lifestyle choices that are birthed out of a need to satisfy perverted inclinations brought on by the very same abuse. The same devil that drove the man or the woman to be inappropriate with the child is the same devil that makes this child, now an adult; act out the same abusive actions and language on others. Abuse creates a sense of normalcy in chaos for the abuse victim. Love, care and affection is misconstrued as abnormal and in some warped way it may be even seen as a sign of weakness. Abuse victims and abusers must be taught what true love is. Love is simply what love does.

To aid an abuser in his recovery from a lifestyle of abuse one must begin with addressing the anger. First, the ability of anger to take control of an individual's life and bear fruit that is not only harmful to them, but all those associated to them must be dealt with. The wisdom text of Proverbs declares that *he who is slow to anger is better than the mighty and he who rules his spirit than he who takes a city.* The abuser must be taught that his anger is what's in control when he or she snaps. He or she must be informed that their emotions and their spirit are driving their lives on a collision course with destruction. A fit of anger that leaves one disoriented and unclear of the original reason for the outburst is a clear indication that your anger has gotten the better of you.

Many abusers will try to rationalize their behavior as being a reasonable reaction to a great injustice shown to them. But they must be educated to the fact that anger does not always have to lead to destructive and disruptive behavior especially if their diagnosis of it is reasonable. How can it be reasonable if you are panting and speaking disjointedly with your heart throbbing and no really sensible thoughts are going through your mind? Paul in his epistle to the church at Ephesus implores us to be angry and do not sin (Ephesians 4:26). It requires that we do not allow wrath to simmer because that gives occasion for the enemy to introduce thoughts of retribution, and revenge. A mind that is seething with anger like a steaming cauldron is an inviting soup for sin to make entrance. Vengeful thinking intimates that one is spiritually immature and lacks understanding of the power structure of human life itself. It's not our job to exact revenge on others because of a perceived wrong. It's God's obligatory duty to even the score.

An abuser has to be told that before them is set a daily battery of choices. Their choices will indicate what part of them is in control, or what parts still hold sway due to their inward desires. Life and death, blessing and cursing, and peace or strife are choices set before us daily. We control what we choose and after making a choice we have to live with the understanding that the choice consequently will control us.

The all-encompassing consequences of abuse are the development of attitudes of discouragement, doubt and fear. A victim of abuse is put into a place of perpetual discouragement. Before, during and after an act of abuse a victim endures discouragement. Their esteem is assaulted, and their sense of value suffers great depreciation. Every human being has a period, or maybe even a season in their life when they have to cope with lowliness, insecurity, hurt and frustration. But imagine that being your constant experience. The abused constantly receives the message that they are not important, and what they're going through really doesn't matter to anyone. They are told that whom they are is inconsequential and what they are going to become is worthless. These messages must be counteracted. An equal or greater measure of encouragement must be sent their way. The victim must be told that they are better than how they may feel, look or even think. They must be told that they're definitely better than their abuser says that they are.

They can find solace in the scripture found in Isaiah the forty-first chapter.

*So do not fear, for I am with you; do not be dismayed, for I am your God. I will strengthen you and help you; I will uphold you with my righteous right hand.*

*For I am the Lord, your God, who takes hold of your right hand and says to you, do not fear; I will help you.*

Those who have been abused or are being abused are on the devil's hit list. He is determined to cause you to believe that your problem is insurmountable. He wants you to think that the likelihood of you coming out whole is slim to none. His plan is to make them choose defeat without putting up a fight, and all he has to do is push them into a corner. But even in the midst of abuse we've got to have the mindset that says God will never put in too small a place or situation for me to grow in. That's what happens in the midst of abuse. We enter a tight place and we feel that there is no escape and that any minute now we will viciously react or simply collapse. There is yet another choice. You can change your situation by first changing your perspective, and you change your perspective by seeing your situation of abuse as a place of growth. And as you grow to fill out that tight place you're being formed to the glory of God. And after its all over, because it shall end, you shall be better, wiser and stronger.

Finally, God knows what you are going through, and wants to help you to get out of it. But in order for God to help you have to show that you want the help. God will never take you out of a predicament that you don't desire a release from. He'll never force his will upon you. He gives you the option of calling His will to past in your life.

# The Dusk of Mankind and the Dawn of the Kingdom

## Chapter Four

## Lest We Stumble

*Now unto Him who is able to keep you from falling, and to present you faultless before the presence of his glory with exceeding joy.*

Jude 24

Be careful for nothing. The kingdom life is a life of watchfulness and attention to detail. It is a deliberate life that requires us to not allow anything to slip by unnoticed. Progress in the kingdom life is predicated on us carefully planning every move because if we fail to plan, we plan to fail. It takes no initiative to fail. You can fail simply by not showing up. We can fail simply by forfeiture. But victory or success depends on a well-executed plan. A. Philip Randolph, the great labor union leader of the American past once said, "Freedom is never given, it is won!" The freedom that is for us and which lies deep in the things of God requires that we position ourselves for victory. Edmund Burke,

## The Dusk of Mankind and the Dawn of the Kingdom

the British theologian of the 17th century said that the only thing necessary for the triumph of evil is for good men to do nothing.

The chaos that is life for the unbeliever should be nothing more than a challenge for the believer. It should not be categorized as a crisis. However, if we call it a challenge, then we're on the right track. It's a challenge to us because human life in the state that it is right now depends a great deal on our sensuality. Originally man was created to operate in life from a place of spirituality. We were created as spirit beings housed in sensitive flesh. But after the initial failure of the first man, and the corruption that followed; God's intent for us to live from the spirit perspective was switched. We started to live according to our sensuality; and our spirituality suffered. Adam and Eve lived originally from a spiritual perspective but after the deception and the fall they became sensual recognizing their nakedness-a reality that prior to the fall was part of their life but not important to their life.

As sensual beings we miss an entire facet of our existence and that is the spiritual dimension within which we live, move and have our being. We don't just live in the physical world; we also live in the spiritual world. Just as we walk by, stand by, sit by and run by numerous individuals in our physical surroundings, believe it or not, we occupy a spiritual dimension that probably has us making a lot more encounters of which we have little awareness. Imagine that, there are probably more spiritual beings that we come into contact with on a daily basis than they are physical people that we meet. If this proposition is to be held as factual then that means that a significant part of how I feel about a thing, or how I feel about a given situation may be due to the effect of my spiritual surroundings.

With this new knowledge about who I am, now I can understand why it is necessary for me to be guarded about what I allow to influence my daily experience. I've got to be careful about what I allow to enter the gateways to my soul. I've got to be cautious about what I tap into and what I allow to tap into me. This is because some of the things that I'm unable to recognize because of their spiritual nature may be operating against me.

    We've talked so far about facing the facts of a contradictory life, killing the giant called, Fear, and running on empty. The next level of kingdom actualization is taking careful notice of the dimension that we usually take the least notice of-the spirit realm. The spirit realm is probably more densely occupied than even our physical environment. When the bible speaks of spiritual warfare it is difficult many times for us to understand the magnitude of its presence in our very midst. It's easy for us to picture military conflict between warring factions and nations on visible terra firma. But it is ultimately difficult to see military-style conflict going on in the spirit realm somewhere around us. Some of us have been unknowingly utilized, recruited and manipulated by this spiritual battle waged in our vicinity. Think about it. The times when you were awoken in the middle of the night in cold sweat, convinced that what you saw in your dream while in a semi-conscious state was really taking place? Or how about the times when you were alone but you couldn't help but feel that there was someone else or something else occupying your very space?

    There is an invisible realm operating around us, and occupying the same space as the visible realm. This invisible spirit realm although unseen exercises great influence on our visible world. It controls how we see our world, how we react to its challenges and even how difficult those challenges may be to us. Scores of us live our lives and never pay attention to the invisible, and we essentially miss the spirit of God's significance in forming and fixing our very existence. While even more of us disregard the spiritual and end up stumbling headlong into deception.

For many of us the first realization that we have a spiritual side to us is when we take our first steps of salvation. We realize that the act of hearing a Word from God had more to it than just a literal auditory occurrence. We know this because prior to salvation, prior to us hearing the Word of God we had heard many things. We heard fairy tales, we heard words of encouragement and discouragement, we heard good news and bad but none of these words had the power to initiate a transformation within us. None of these words spoken to us and heard with our natural ears had the ability to make us believe. Therefore, when we heard the Word of God there had to be something that took place in the spiritual realm that sparked life into our spirit; because it was our spirit man that heard the voice of the Father in the text, and as a result earned us faith.

Salvation revives the spirit man but sanctification sustains him. What are the ways in which we consciously enter the spirit realm? What can we do as sensual beings to reverse the trend and become spiritual beings? When dealing with our dual nature and attempting to strike a balance we must keep a key concept in mind. It says that whatever you focus on, you will feed, and consequently whatever you feed will grow.

Prior to having any spiritual self-conception we focused on nourishing satisfying and meeting the basic needs of our physical bodies. As a result of this focus our flesh grew not necessarily in size only but mainly it grew in influence. We gave our lives over to the needs of our physical body. We were figuratively living to eat rather than moderately eating to live. We literally surrendered to the longings of our eyes, ears, noses, skin and tongues. Our senses ruled the roost.

Salvation is more a spiritual experience than it is a physical one, and in order for us to stay consistent in it we must acquire some spiritual sensitivity. If we try to do this walk of salvation completely in the physical we will surely fail. Our spiritual man has to be focused on and fed so that he might not only come alive but that he might grow in strength and influence over our lives. Fleshly thinking is what has gotten man into trouble with his conception of sexuality, marriage, lack of good health and immoral practices. Spiritual thinking is the only way for some of us to come out of deviant behavior.

Some clear examples of how we've been pigging out in the natural is the fact that activities that are purely physically satisfying have become wholly acceptable and almost as a way of life. These were once practices although done by some, were seen as taboo or out of the ordinary by most. However, today substance abuse is now seen as almost a rite of passage for a challenging adolescent life. There is also this widespread sentiment among the male culture that the viewing of pornography is a part of the natural progression from boyhood to manhood. Some sectors of society in an effort to explain a growing trend of individuals identifying with homosexuality, as their lifestyle and at younger and younger ages, have come to the conclusion that everyone knowingly or unknowingly goes through a phase of changing sexual preference or identity. Even the deplorable practice of pedophilia that has gone through its own metamorphosis in terms of its widespread public acceptance is becoming a daily issue on the evening news. These are all consequences and effects of a culture given over to the needs, desires, and inclinations of its fleshly carnal nature. A spiritual awakening is what's needed in our culture. The Bible talks of a time when mankind would begin to consider evil good and good evil. We seem to be living in that very time, when we consider the degree to which deviant behavior is being defended. When we find ourselves helpless to change impulsive and addictive behavior that is harmful to us, we are a spiritually dead people.

How can we get more spiritual? How can we reverse the trend and do our part to create a spiritual reawakening in this land? It all begins with the foundational spiritual disciplines of prayer and fasting. In order to live a kingdom life we must earnestly practice the spiritual disciplines because it is in these disciplines that we equip ourselves to fight the pending and inevitable resistance in our flesh. Physical discipline may work in some circumstances and under certain constraints but if those constraints are removed the human flesh will immediately return to the old familiar way. But if we adopt spiritual discipline we in turn strengthen our spirit, and will eventually bring our fleshly, *soulish* self subject to our spirit. Our victory is predicated on putting our flesh under and pushing our spirit over the top.

Why are prayer and fasting considered spiritual rather than physical disciplines? Prayer and fasting are both physical actions that we take but they render spiritual results. In each discipline a physical practice is brought under studied control by exertion of our will, and in any spiritual exercise some sort of physical loss must be experienced. When we pray we are relying on something that is completely outside of the natural minds comprehension. We utter words into the atmosphere and sometimes it may just be uttered in our conscience not even out loud but we believe that they are heard in the heavenlies. Prayer is a gateway for God to enter into our lives, and influence who we are and who we are to become. If I never pray I never give God access to my problems. Prayer is an amalgamation of praise and petition in a personal setting. I am approaching God in my secret place so that He may intervene in my public crises. It is when we personally approach God to not only thanking Him but also to profess our faith in Him to achieve all that we purposed in our hearts to ask him about. Prayer literally seals a spiritual agreement of trust between God and us. It acts as a channel through which our soulish and physical actions ushers the power of God into our affairs. Fasting is a starving of the physical self so that the spiritual self might be awoken. It should be done in concert with consecration and time dedicated to meditation on God's Word. This joint activity is necessary because it restricts the physical while loosing the spiritual. Prayer and fasting closes the gap between where we are and where God is, and hence where God would have us to be.

You may be reading this chapter and finding these ideas difficult to comprehend. That is understandable, especially if you consider the fact that your entire life has been driven by your senses. Most of us have been thought that if we can't see it we shouldn't believe it, and that teaching has been engrained into our psyche in such a way that for us to depend on an invisible God to manifest change in our visible lives has been a great challenge for many of us to overcome. The

## The Dusk of Mankind and the Dawn of the Kingdom

Book of Romans in the eighth chapter tells us that the carnal mind is enmity against God: for it is not subject to the law of God, neither indeed can be. That tells me that my natural mind could never, and would never be able to comprehend the spirit realm. However, I can stand in the consolation that understanding is not necessary for God's power to be made manifest in my life. Rather, I simply have to believe. I simply have to bring my heart to a place of belief and trust in God to deliver the goods even if I can't understand how.

A spiritual rebirth is necessary in our lives or else we'll be unable to prevent ourselves from falling again into the trap of sin. Jesus told Nicodemus unless a man is born of water and of the Spirit; unless he is born from above he cannot enter into the kingdom of God. As we endeavor to enter the kingdom-literally the way of righteousness-we must first take on a position of standing in the spirit. Entrance into the kingdom is only given to that which is spiritual. Jesus declared that spiritual sight was a necessity for us to even see His kingdom dominion at work. I'll always be blind to the kingdom's influence if I continually live according to my flesh. If I allow emotional impulse to rule my decision making in this life I will continually abort my spiritual access. Unregenerate sight lacks the ability to comprehend, see or sense an ever-present spiritual God. God will forever be near them but yet still out of their reach. He's closer than they presently think, and more aware of their issues than they could even understand.

*The wind blows wherever it pleases. You hear its sound, but you cannot tell where it comes from or where it is going. So it is with everyone born of the Spirit.*
John 3:8 (NIV)

When we are born again according to the Spirit we obtain supernatural power to operate in the invisible realm. We earn access, influence and power to speak into the atmosphere and cause things to change, move and appear out of nowhere, just like the ability of the wind to affect the atmosphere in which we live. Spiritual rebirth gives us the god type of power *to speak those things that are not as though they were.*

## *Kingdom Keys* **on Staying the Course**

Where and when do we begin to stay the course on this life of kingdom advancement? It begins with being grounded in the things that concern our eternal existence. Much of our lives up to this juncture has involved procuring the necessities to simply make in the temporal. We prayed simply to get our needs met in the here and now. We read the bible just to understand a little more about whom we are, and we praised God for sustaining us in this temporary life. But, what do we do with everything else that we learn about our relationship with God, and our duty as citizens of the kingdom?

What do we do with the ensuing trouble that seems to be engulfing our lives the further we move in the things of God and the more we grow in trusting His Word and His will toward us? We've got to stay the course at all cost. We've got to develop a life that is literally soaked in prayer. As simple as that may sound, prayer is still an area of great difficulty in its exercise for believers.

Prayer is an area in which many believers underestimate the legitimacy and efficacy of its work. Many still see prayer as just an exercise in futility that really has no power to change the circumstances under which we currently live. It is seen as something that is required and spiritually necessary but of no consequence to the natural outlook of our lives. Therefore, when prayer is held in such meager esteem it loses its ability to affect change.

Prayer must be packaged in a spirit of faith, or it is just empty words being uttered into the atmosphere. This is where the breakdown begins. We allow the inconveniences of this life to dictate the level of faith that we will have in Christ. The greater the struggle that we experience in this life the more the foundation of our faith is tried, and henceforth crumbles. We set time limits on our suffering and we determine in our own minds when we will come out. We basically orchestrate the level of our endurance and if God doesn't send deliverance then, we lose faith. Then with every subsequent challenge a little more faith is diminished until we completely lose faith in God to deliver us.

How can we prevent this collapse in trust? We've got to first come to God in faith even in our hour of prayer. Faith grants us access and makes God pay attention to our request. Prayer brings God's heavenly will earthward once it is preceded by faith. You might be asking how can I be assured that my prayer is preceded by faith? All you have to do is determine what God says concerning obtaining faith. In the Bible, the Word of God, it says that faith comes by hearing and hearing, by the Word of God. That means that the faith that I need to trust God literally comes from God, and is vested in his Word. The Word of God does two things. It activates my hearing, giving me spiritual discernment and revelation, and secondly it deposits faith into my conscience. It both causes me to hear God properly and then once I'm able to hear God properly it then gives me faith through its words to believe God for my salvation, deliverance and empowerment.

What does that mean for my "staying the course"? It means that I must therefore become a student of God's Word. My daily life should in some way have the practice of reading, marking and inwardly digesting the Word of God. As I daily read and study the Word I will grow in spiritual understanding and stamina. Staying the course despite the collapse of all that is around us is all about stamina. It's about developing spiritual stamina. It's about making scripture personally relevant to us. It's about seeing our story in the story of struggle that the characters in the Bible had to endure. It's about having an Adam resolve to go on despite losing the greatest gift that God could have given a man. It's about trusting God like Noah despite never having seen rain. It's about knowing that you are going through an Abram experience after you made the decision to part ways with family and friends. It's about being like Joseph and David and having only God to trust in the darkest hour. That's how we stay the course. When we read the bible and increase our faith by understanding that what God did for those men and women who trusted Him, he can do for us who trust Him today.

Equipping ourselves to stay the course begins with familiarizing ourselves with the Scriptures and then taking those Scriptures and praying to God not only our needs, but also His Word. When we pray God's word back to Him we set forth an obligation on his part to respond to what he already promised and declared. Praying God's Word restores our confidence and it emboldens his fight on our behalf.

## The Dusk of Mankind and the Dawn of the Kingdom

    Though the storms may be raging and the waves beating against our sides, we must believe that God is, and He is a rewarder of them that diligently seek Him. Our diligence is exemplified in our study of His Word. It is doubly displayed in our acts of prayer toward Him. Jesus Christ is the great tug boat that hauls our vessels through the daunting choppy seas of adversity. He is a sure ship that neither bows nor bends to the ensuing wind. As long as we pray, study and trust he will attach himself to our situation and guide us through the jagged obstacles of the sea and bring us to shore to the place of that great lighthouse of God.

# The Dusk of Mankind and the Dawn of the Kingdom

## Chapter Five

## A Deliberate Spirit

*Then said I unto them, Ye see the distress that we are in, how Jerusalem lieth waste, and the gates thereof are burned with fire: come, and let us build up the wall of Jerusalem, that we be no more a reproach.*

*Then I told them of the hand of my God which was good upon me; as also the king's words that he had spoken unto me. And they said, Let us rise up and build. So they strengthened their hands for this good work.*
Nehemiah 2:17,18

You must be a kingdom-minded individual. You haven't lost interest in what you've read thus far and that means that you mean business about causing God's kingdom to come to pass in this time. I'm excited that you've chosen to continue on this journey of discovery in the ways that you could act as a conduit for the kingdom of God to be made manifest in this world. Ultimately, every human being in their own way is seeking a way in which they could contribute to the ever-approaching time of decision. That time is when

## The Dusk of Mankind and the Dawn of the Kingdom

every knee shall bow and every tongue confesses that Jesus Christ is Lord. Some may argue that they do not believe in such a time, and therefore their lives are not focused on any such pursuit. However, regardless of ones conclusions to the contrary, be it walking by faith or by fate we all are marching to a final destination. Our souls consciously or unconsciously are assuming positions of belief or unbelief in a soon coming king, and these are positions that we will have to deal with the consequences of when the time comes.

If you've read this far you understand the perspective that I am coming from. It is one that prescribes to the belief that Jesus, the well-known, earthly son of a carpenter, born in a small insignificant town in Israel called Bethlehem, and raised in the nearby village of Nazareth was and is the Lord and savior of mankind. I don't believe that he was just an extraordinary man who happened to publicly live a spotless life and aid many in the miraculous curing of ailments and the healing of dysfunctional relationships, but I believe that he was the savior of the world long alluded to in the old testament scriptures.

Every type and shadow including the articles to the tabernacle, the manna from heaven, the water out of the rock, and the sacrificial lamb among others were made a reality in him. All other arguments to the contrary such as why did he have to be Jewish and other cultural-specific arguments are just that, arguments that lack solid merit. Jesus' Jewish heritage as divisive as it may seem and downright as offensive as it may be for some who find it hard to subscribe to a messiah of a Semitic background should be the last factor one considers in accepting the stance of his divinity. Belief from a spiritual perspective requires that we look beyond the minimalist framework of race.

Race as it stands is a social construct that has done more to divide us than to truly celebrate us. Our differences have more often than necessary been used to assign levels of significance and value rather than affording all equal worth-while highlighting uniqueness. And unfortunately even in church this has become an ideology that threatens to keep the body of Christ divided sharply along racial boundaries.

However, I believe that the only way that Sunday mornings can lose the dubious distinction of being the most segregated day of the week is for the church to open its eyes to its own error of exclusion. The reason I am taking the time out in this chapter to even address the issue of racial separation within the church is because this kingdom advance, the crux of this text, cannot be accomplished by a divided church. The old guard notions of a black church, white church or even an Asian church are just that, old school notions that bare no weight or value in the kingdom of God. The kingdom of God is not a kingdom that is identifiable by racial distinctions. It is not a kingdom that is defined by social status but rather it is a kingdom that crosses all social and racial boundaries and includes every spectrum of society.

We talked before about how the kingdom cogitates away from the idea of independence and self-dependence. Working alone in the kingdom we can do nothing. An exclusively black church or an exclusively white church aiming to effectively change the sentiment of society toward a loving God will lack validation because the picture that it would portray either way would be one of exclusion and one that unavoidably would bring opposition. However, together our minds would fuse into something that could overcome any cultural barriers that would limit a race-specific

# The Dusk of Mankind and the Dawn of the Kingdom

movement. Unity in the body of Christ across racial barriers and social status creates a power that is far beyond that of the separate parts. A united church would be more powerful than a united white church or a united black church. The kingdom cannot be found alone, and we who are in the kingdom cannot find ourselves alone. Jesus said the kingdom is inside of us. Together we can find that hidden kingdom and overcome the devil of this world.

We are in a season right now in human history when the barriers between the disparate social groups in society are gradually being dissolved. At this time in American history there are more areas in which there is commonality of purpose and vision across the races than ever before. We are finally seeing real gains being made by minority groups when it concerns economic empowerment than ever before. Real change for the better in American societal class structure is evident today in the number of people considered minorities who hold positions of influence, both politically, and economically in this country. However, there is still room for added change and development.

Many of us up to this moment in our lives have gone through life from trial to test, to trial to test and at each turn we've been driven down a course simply as a result of the obstacles that have been placed in our way. If we were to really examine our personal history's we would find that many of the decisions we've made were decisions that we felt that we had to make. Outside of the simple decisions like what outfit we would like to wear or what channel we would like to watch the destiny decisions that have directed our lives were many times made not because of what may ultimately be of the greatest benefit to us but rather were decisions that we were forced into.

Many of the issues with regard to what we lack in finances, in relationships, in security, in education, in peace and in possessions—stems from decisions that we felt we were cornered into making. The debt that we face today—that car, that wide-screen television, that outfit, that Credit Card and that loan all were decisions that we made hastily and on impulse. We made some purchases in the past just to please a mate, or a child or even an enemy. We bought things that we thought would keep people in our lives. We bought things that we thought would show others that we loved them.

We pursued relationships because everyone else was doing it. Some of you even started dating certain people out of a sense of pity. This man has been pursuing me for so long and I've been coming up empty for so long I might as well give him a chance. We've been in a cycle of settling for that which we didn't really want but what we believed was the only thing we could afford.

Many of us are stuck in the middle of an uncomfortable situation. We've stood at the altar hearing the Pastor say, "Do you take this woman or do you take this man?" Then we've closed our ears, shut our eyes, swallowed deeply and said, "I do!" Only then do we realize that what we've signed up for is not what we really wanted. Our lives have been bound and driven by the decisions and feelings of other men.

We haven't pursued higher education because we believed that going to college was something that wasn't for us. There are so many of us who have settled for less just because somehow we felt that society dictated that we should settle for little. But this is your time to change that sentiment. You've got to develop a

# The Dusk of Mankind and the Dawn of the Kingdom

deliberate spirit. No longer will you let life happen to you. No longer will you go left because of the press. But you shall live life with a purpose, and you shall live life according to what God says.

When we live our lives according to the beck and call of men we put ourselves in the precarious position of depending on uncertain power. We leave ourselves open to error. We limit ourselves to the turning tides of the times. Never let another man assume the status of God in your life. Never let another man control how you think, act and certainly how you believe because men are not equipped to properly cradle another human soul.

We've got to begin to live life deliberately. We've got to speak those things that are not, as though they were. We've got to take hold of the power that's in the tongue. The Bible says that, "Life and death are in the power of the tongue." That means that within your tongue there's power not only to give life but also to take it away.

When we live unfocused lives where our emotions are untrammeled and we do that which is simply pleasing to our senses we are living surrendered lives. A surrendered life isn't necessarily a bad place to be in but the key is to figure out what we are surrendered to. A life surrendered to the whim and fancy of other men or women is a life heading for catastrophe because men and women cannot be trusted for the welfare of another individual. Only God can be trusted in that arena. Only the spirit of God can faithfully sustain a human soul. Another human soul will merely do for that other soul whatever brings pleasure and satisfaction to itself. The only one benefiting from the experience would be the human soul that has control.

A deliberate life is a blessed life. A deliberate life is a life in which our actions are purposefully directed toward seeing the establishment of God's will in the atmosphere. Martin Luther King Jr. once said, "If you stand for nothing, you'll fall for anything." A deliberate life is one that stands on something. It is a life that is committed to a cause.

*Watch ye stand fast in the faith, quit you like men, be strong.*

1 Corinthians 16:13

He who stands fast in the faith is convicted regarding his relationship with God. He who not only trusts but has a holy fervor for the things of God—born of faith and deeply entrenched in it, the bible says that he would be like a tree planted by the waters. Standing fast in faith is to be rooted and unmoved in ones dependence on God's direction and provision. Even when the storms and the waves of adversity beat against your parts even the more shall you stand still.

The standing still that is characteristic of a deliberate spirit is not a stance of inactivity. It requires positioning ourselves with such a posture that though we may be crouched low under adversity, and disappointment, beaten on every side we are not knocked over. Living life with purpose requires a deliberate spirit. This type of spirit demands power from God. One who's deliberate in the life that they live must develop a connection with the power source because without it our deliberation is in vain.

What is a deliberate spirit? It is one that is determined, focused on a goal, assured in his walk and ready to accept responsibility for his actions. A

# The Dusk of Mankind and the Dawn of the Kingdom

deliberate spirit attracts both allies and enemies. Allies come because they recognize that their destiny is tied into your determination. They realize that they must connect with your courage because you have created a momentum that is pressing toward God. Your allies have noticed that you have set your face against the enemy and toward God. It is difficult not to notice a deliberate spirit; because determination dismantles the obstacles of fear. A deliberate spirit empowers and encourages those who would normally shrink back in fear. The bible says that God has not given us a spirit of fear but of power, and of love and of a sound mind.

Enemies come alongside a deliberate spirit because they understand that with the backing of a deliberate spirit you will not settle for defeat. They may hate you, and it is really that they hate who they see you becoming but they can't help aligning with you because they see progress. They see you attaining to places that they desire to reach. Their hatred is a hatred that is deeply vested in envy. They envy where God is taking you. The enemy realizes that the advantage that they once had over you was lost when a deliberate spirit overtook you.

As we advance in this kingdom battle we've got to make some declarations. The first declaration should be that we will not stand back in fear again. We faced our fears in the second chapter of this book and now we are gaining forward momentum in this kingdom walk. The second declaration should be that we are not going to settle for less. Our motto has to become "good is an enemy of better!" I've got to do more than just what's good. I've got to do that which is best for my family and I. The next declarations should be ones of affirmation of the power that I already possess. It should be that I have the power to change. I have the power to challenge my current situation. I have the power to choose another path. I have the power to proclaim into the atmosphere where I'm determined to end up.

Kingdom speech, or declarative speech as I would like to refer to it, is the epitome of proclaiming the conditions that I wish to exist within. As long as I am speaking what God said, I am affirming his good and perfect will not only for my life but also for my world. Therefore, I must not only be declarative about who I am and where I desire to be but I must make sure that it echoes what God already said. That is where the power lies. The power doesn't lie in who relays the message but rather in the originator of the message. When I speak those things that are not as though they are, I am simply relaying into action what God spoke thousands of years ago. When God made promises to Abraham, Isaac, Jacob and Moses among others he was speaking to me. As long as I am in earshot of those spoken declarations they are referring to my situation as well. His words are not just logos, script that brings knowledge but it is also *rhema* word that is food and brings life.

The determinative character of my deliberate spirit does not stop with how I speak over my life but it also continues with how, when and what I communicate to God. I'm determined because I pray. I have daily communion with God both formally and informally as I quietly contemplate every circumstance and situation asking God's advice here and there. And in my prayer I received assurance from God. Prayer is a bipolar experience. It must include transmission to him but also we need to be receptive to his response.

Too often we approach God in prayer, and we lay out a list of request or issues and concerns and we get

## The Dusk of Mankind and the Dawn of the Kingdom

up from our knees without even waiting for a reply. Many of us chalk up the entire exchange to an act of reminding God of what we're going through and then he'll focus his attention your way after you've, as it were, sent him a reminder. Prayer has become a way of dropping God reminders about us rather than entering into a real exchange and conversation.

The bible says whatsoever things ye desire when ye pray, believe that ye receive them, and ye shall have them. What a powerful statement about the significance of prayer. In prayer we can get solid evidentiary assurance that our faithful act will bear fruit. Prayer triggers faith. It is a faith that emanates from the very presence of God and connects with us in prayer and creates in us a faith that, believes but also realizes, appropriates and takes. It gives us a super-faith. After I pray about it my mind is overtaken by a realized certainty even if I can't see it, I know it.

As I develop a deliberate spirit, determined to live within the kingdom of God as a viable, effective and fruitful citizen of that kingdom I must arm myself in prayer. My determination to succeed must come in my times of prayer. Determination is the sense of assurance that that which I'm pursuing is virtually mine, it's just a matter of time, and it's just a matter of positioning. Prayer creates the assurance because it is backed by an all-powerful source.

Along with the determination not to give up, the character of being focused on a goal can identify the deliberate spirit. The deliberate spirit in its stubborn resolve is not a "determined fool" but rather is led by a goal rather than driven by impulse. We talked previously about the dangers of impulsive thinking and acting and we know that uncontrolled determination can lead to destruction but this deliberate spirit is led by a goal. Impulse is usually a result of being channeled toward several foci at once. This is counterproductive in the kingdom. Our focus should be on one goal, God.

The deliberate spirit makes the individual put one foot forward today expecting that it lands in there promised tomorrow. We look unto Jesus, the author and the finisher of our faith. He set the example and laid the groundwork of which any approach that I make must follow. The bible said, "Who for the joy that was set before him endured the cross, despising the shame and is set down at the right hand of the throne of God. As there was joy set before Jesus, I have to believe that there is joy set before me. This knowledge keeps me going and able to deal with the shame that others will inevitably direct upon me.

Our goal as a deliberate spirit is to focus on God's guidance. Many of us come up short of the mark and miss opportunities to benefit from God's power because our eyes are set on the wrong things. We are focused on our faults. We sit and we contemplate ways that we can make ourselves right. We look at our circumstances. We examine our finances. We set our sights on a scheme or a plan that we think will get us out of what we've stumbled into. Our lack of determination has concurrently caused us to stumble into habits and idiosyncrasies that cause us to focus on what we've done wrong.

However, God continues to stand above the fray and declare that we should look unto him and focus on him. Set your faith on where you should be and not on where you currently stand. God placed your eyes in the front of your head, and on the top portion of your face because you were made to be constantly looking forward, pressing ahead and keeping your head up. You can only turn your head back partially and for a moment because retrospect is supposed to be a momentary action. God did not make you the way he did so that you can use you the way you please- there is a plan and purpose for everything. Stop looking back longer than you need to. Look back, take account of where you came from, and then turn your head and focus on your future.

We've discussed thus far that a deliberate spirit is determined to finish the course, focused on a single goal and the next character trait that we need to pay attention is that of an assured walk. My walk as a deliberate spirit is assured by the intent and the purpose behind my advance. The Bible says, "We walk by faith, and not by sight."(2 Corinthians 5:7) It is an assured walk not grounded in what we see but in what we know God is able to do. Having faith is having a secure knowledge in God's ability to produce. Faith without works is dead. Possessing faith without practicing that faith is an oxymoron. Faith that isn't worked out in our lives soon exits our life. Faith evaporates unless it's being empowered to work in our lives.

One of the greatest mistakes we make as believers is that we take faith for granted. We many times deflate the impact of faith in our lives by limiting our understanding of it to simple belief. Faith is more than just belief but rather is belief pumped up on steroids. It allows you to see and consider one able to achieve that which others will swear is impossible. Faith must be worked out in diligence and perseverance. Diligence in planning and preparation of your desired destiny, and perseverance in seeing your plan come to past.

Abraham the father of the faithful walked with an assurance that was rooted in having a deliberate spirit. The bible teaches us that by faith Abraham when he was called to go out into a place that he should after receive for an inheritance, obeyed; and he went out, not knowing whither he went. He did not see it with his natural eyes. He did not even know where it was. But all he depended upon was the call and the promise of God. God has called you and made some promises to you. Are you willing to walk forward simply on that call, and on that word? Abraham illustrated implicit faith, and obedience toward God, the only one to whom such faith was due. We need to do the same, with the word and promise that God has made to us.

We can only know that word and promise that is specific to us if we maintain a personal line of communication and relation with God. It won't come by just memorizing scripture. It won't come by just attending church. It won't come by just joining an auxiliary or establishing a ministry and doing Christian work but it comes by having relationship with God. Relationship comes through communication and intimacy. God is waiting to endow you with a deliberate spirit if you would endow him with praise, adoration and worship.

After I've gained determination, focused on a goal, walked with a divine assurance then I'm called, we are called to take responsibility for that which results from our actions. Everything that happens to us because of our deliberate spirit will ultimately be to our benefit. It's easier for us to accept responsibility when the outcome is wrought in righteousness. Responsibility is a severely difficult task when our initial act was in error and disobedience. Responsibility is the culminating

## The Dusk of Mankind and the Dawn of the Kingdom

character trait of one who has matured into living life with a deliberate spirit.

Responsibility is the mark of one who has been through something and realizes what part they played in their own complacencies. Young men and women find it hard to take responsibility for their lives because they often believe that they have not yet experienced enough failure or success because of the personal decisions that they have made. Many young people feel no need for taking responsibility because much of their lives are controlled, directed and guided by others. Therefore, responsibility is inconsequential and irrelevant to their existence. But those of you who live not at the command and the control of parents are in a position not only to take control of your lives but more importantly to take responsibility for your lives.

The bible says, "When I was a child I acted as a child but now I've become a man, and I put away childish things." God is saying there are too many men and women walking around and acting like kids who lack control of their attitudes, urges and desires. And God is saying today is the day that you will walk as a man, or as a woman and occupy the place and the posture of one who has a deliberate spirit.

Stop blaming others. Stop blaming your wife, or your girlfriend for enabling your immaturity. Stop blaming your husband or your boyfriend for keeping you back. Stop blaming the government, and the system, and the man, for your inability to make financial ends meet. Stop blaming society, television and cable networks for the corrupted morals of your children. Stop blaming the school system for your child's inability to learn and behave like he or she has some common sense. Stop blaming the streets for your wayward sons and daughters.

Adopt a deliberate spirit. Get on your knees, listen to his voice and set your eyes on Him. Digest his Word, and walk with your chest high and your eyes focused on the Son.

We have to understand that even with a deliberate spirit it isn't easy. Adversity does not decrease with a deliberate spirit but our ability to deal with difficulty increases. We have to believe and know that the sun is still shining somewhere behind the dark clouds of an ensuing storm that I currently see. My senses may see distress and a rising storm but my deliberate spirit senses the delivering power of God getting ready to come the moment I call on the name of Jesus.

The fact that I can see anything tells me that the sun is shining on the other side of this. Without the sun's light emanating around us continually as we exist on this planet I would be blind to the possibility of future victory. But I've got a Godly resolve that says that I know that my redeemer lives and He sits on high watching and enabling me through his Spirit to cause his kingdom to come, just like the instruction for prayer says. Thy kingdom come on earth as it is in heaven.

*Kingdom Keys* **on having a Deliberate Spirit**
A deliberate spirit is one that is committed to the cause. How do you determine whether you are committed to the cause? Examine your thinking. How do you think about the obstacles that confront you on a daily basis? Not what do you think about, but rather how do you think about these obstacles?

# The Dusk of Mankind and the Dawn of the Kingdom

Do you measure the size of the bill? Are you daily pulling out your statements and trying to calculate how much you will need to contribute to each weekly so as to bring them down to a manageable amount and still seeing no way out? Are you trying to carry the weight of your family problems, school issues, and community issues on your own shoulders? Maybe that is the problem.

It takes little effort in this life to lose heart over what appears to be completely out of our control. But what about if we looked at these circumstances and see that God is still in control? We are only able to see that God is in control, if we are resting in Him. If we remain residing in His shadow, then and only then, will we see that he is greater than any mountain, or obstacle, or debt, or issue, or problem that we may be facing today.

Let us recap what a deliberate spirit entails:
- Being determined –This comes thru prayer, seeking God's voice and direction.

**Reference scriptures**: Num. 13:26-31, Num. 14:1-9, 1 Sam. 14:1-5, 2 Kings 2:1-6, Esther 4:10-16, Acts 6:8-7:60

- Focused on a goal  -This comes thru setting one's eyes on Jesus. Learning of his testimony and his lifestyle, and how he spoke and why he did what he did. That comes thru studying the scriptures.

**Reference scriptures**: Phil. 3:12-14, 1 Cor. 9:24,25

- Assured in walk  -This comes by being planted in the Word. Solidly standing up for what is right in God's eyes. Being a beacon, a role model of integrity and a forthright representative of the kingdom agenda.

**Reference scriptures**: 1 John 1:7; 3 John 3,4; Col. 2:6; Gal. 5:16, 25; 1 John 2:6; Eph. 4:1; Eph. 5:15; 1 Thess. 4:1

- Ready to accept responsibility - This comes with spiritual maturity. Discovering ones place or niche in the kingdom. Prayer, prayer and more prayer, is the only answer for entrance into this dimension of walking with God.

**Reference scriptures**: John 9:39-41; John 15:22, 24; Matt. 11:20-24

# The Dusk of Mankind and the Dawn of the Kingdom

## Chapter Six

## Rebel, with a Cause

*But they rebelled, and vexed his Holy Spirit: therefore he was turned to be their enemy, and he fought against them.*

Isaiah 63:10

Misdirected rebellion is the core cause of social disorder among the younger generation of today. Young people eager to throw off the chains of conformity dive headlong into causes that lack significance. Our culture is inundated with images of young people obsessed with fame, engaged in debauchery and generally concerned only for their personal comfort. As I was growing up I remember the term used rather negatively by the adults in my life, "the me generation." Back then it was considered a developmental stage, a phase that all young people went through when the self took precedence over everything else. Now as an adult when I consider the issues and interest of today's youth it appears that the "me generation" phase is slowly becoming a way of life and not just a small part of the self-discovery that takes place on the road to maturity.

# The Dusk of Mankind and the Dawn of the Kingdom

Me generation youth are seen as rebellious trendsetters. They are doing and attempting things. Some of the things they are attempting are risky and others are downright harmful. This is being done all in the name of wanting experience in a myriad of things. A central philosophy of the me generation is that things considered prohibitive by the general public are that way only because the general public is really out of the loop. The risk and harm associated with certain practices is tossed to the wind in the name of pursuing the thrill. The dominating youth culture of today is involved in rebellion without a cause.

Rebellion by young people is nothing new. In some cases that rebellion initiated fundamental, lasting change in the social dynamic of a once dysfunctional social structure. History tells us of episodes of political change for the better in many nations that was driven by the rebellious protest of its younger citizens. Much of the dismantling of communist regimes across Eastern Europe was spurred and under-girded by strong student support from concerned and informed youth. In those cases the unbiased perspective of young people looking to reverse the prejudice and injustice they saw being perpetrated by the older generation was a promising indicator of society's future outlook. Even today, a few influential and devoted young people spearhead most of society's humanitarian causes.

The fight to increase the awareness of the HIV/AIDS crisis in the continent of Africa, the war against poverty, the campaign against the genocide in Darfur, and the fight to feed the hungry of this nation and much of the Third World are all causes that have wide base of college and even high school age activist.

However, these shining examples are the exception and regrettably not the rule.

As an educator, I daily come into contact with young people. The overarching concern among them seems to be that of acceptance by both peers and adults. Being that as it may I have found that the primary acceptance that they strive for is actually that of their peers. The desire for acceptance often manifests itself in these young people making choices, forming alliances and taking stands just because others have also done it. They make choices to ditch class based on the decision of the dominant personality in the peer group. Young people form alliances with the most unlikely characters just because it is seen as the "in thing" to do. This is done sometimes even at the cost of some young people forsaking long held personal, familial and even cultural mores. The acceptance pull of peers can even over power parentally instilled standards of behavior and normalcy.

They take these stands so that they could evade the label of "square." The most demeaning feeling for a young person between the stages of adolescents and teenage years is to be considered the one who sticks out like a sore thumb. Peer pressure takes on a life of its own, and the individuals caught in its enveloping influence are hardly able to explain why they got involved in the first place.

What does this have to do with the dawning of the kingdom of God? Why is the rebellion of youth a relevant topic within the realm of the kingdom advance? The answer is simple. Without the youth the kingdom lacks a viable, vibrant component that would make the kingdom family incomplete. Churches, believing, fruitful and effective ministry that fails to meet the

# The Dusk of Mankind and the Dawn of the Kingdom

needs of the youngest in society because we believe that they somehow are not mature enough to appreciate the kingdom of God is misguided ministry. How can we expect to keep the idea of salvation viable if everyone that believes is above a certain age? We would then be relegating God's work to those who have attained some level of antiquity. Again this would give young people the impression that Jesus is something to be sought in the twilight years and as long as you're young and full of vigor he is not of any significance.

As the dusk of mankind comes into view and the rays of light of a new coming dawn of the kingdom breaks forth on the horizon the church needs to turn its focus on winning the youngest for Christ at all cost. Even more so relevant are the youth that occupy that between generation that are no longer tiny, impressionable babes but are now young men and women who have been through their share of experiences and can clearly articulate their understanding of who God is or is not to them.

How do we approach the young men and women who are in that rebellious generation, that generation that is struggling to define themselves and make marked distinctions between themselves and their parents? How do we address their needs? How do we recruit them to play their part in building the kingdom of God in the earth? It begins with attacking what they fear the most, and answering their hardest questions about life, disappointment, dashed dreams and broken promises. Babes may get disappointed sometimes and they may have some promises made to them broken but they get over it because they are babies and they live in the now with little concern for tomorrow and they have too little a past to be concerned about. But what about the teenager who had a rough adolescent childhood who has known only disappointment has no dreams and has never even been made a promise. How do you deal with a young man who says I don't know what I want to be when I grow up because I don't see myself growing up?

These are the young men and women that once only occupied our most depressed communities and saw no way out. But today, we are faced with a part of this generation that has all that a poor child would dream about having and they still have the same sense of doom and inescapable doldrums of an ordinary life. How do you deal with the child who just does not want to be someday considered ordinary? Here again is another reason we see wholesale rebellion without a valid cause. They are rebelling against the idea of slipping into a normal lackluster life that isn't celebrity oriented.

The negative effect of rebellion among young people was once a crisis specific to urban communities. These communities plagued with the problems of poverty, lack of opportunity for upliftment, where the poorest of the poor were redlined to live and placed at the mercy of various economically based incoherencies unlike the rest of society, fostered a youth culture of hopelessness. Young people in these communities saw no chance for themselves to make it out of the ensnarement of poverty, drug abuse and the government solutions of public assistance. Therefore, the ideals of the wider public that espoused pursuing the American dream, and breaking the glass ceiling of corporate advance became ideals to be rebelled against rather than goals to achieve. Urban youth created their own pathways to success. Success was fundamentally reconceptualized in the ways and means to it, while preserving the ends of financial independence. These pathways to success unfortunately included the real

## The Dusk of Mankind and the Dawn of the Kingdom

likelihood of passage through the criminal justice system, the experience of which further tarnished the entire character of the rebellion.

The urban American youth crisis of just a few years ago has mushroomed into a general American youth problem. The brick and mortar walls of our concrete mazes we call the urban inner cities can no longer tightly hold the powder keg of criminal gang activity, and illegal drug use. The issues that held our low income neighborhoods under arrest for years have now become the issues of the suburban soccer mom and white collar employed dad who carpools to work downtown. Today, we have young white males and females forming gangs and wearing the paraphernalia and using the language that was once exclusively part of the urban culture.

There are several people who would argue and outright condemn my next contention concerning the reason for this problematic burgeoning of the borders of this social ill. However, their disagreement does not negate the fact that it is a widespread problem and my contention is a mitigating factor in that problem spreading. Urban America's rehashing of the "big house with the white picket fence" success motif has birthed the powerful offshoot of the pop music culture that we call today, Hip Hop. This movement of sorts grew out of a subculture within poverty-stricken African American neighborhoods where creativity, black consciousness, racial upliftment and outlets for culturally specific expression coalesced to create a language, style of dress and musical genre that drew on the idea of rebellion.

The Hip Hop culture in its infancy focused on the musical expression, the dance and the language used in the musical renditions. This was a language that literally became its own linguistic code for the streets. The music despite offering pockets of social commentary on the difficult life in our urban ghettos still focused on the party experience. It allowed for the performers and the audience to transcend the deplorable conditions of the life within often rat and roach infested apartment buildings, and still enjoy life.

However, with growing popularity, and wider acceptance as a viable vehicle for directing the youth culture, the message in the music, language and lifestyle shifted. As the psychology of subjection changed in these communities and record executives realized that the musical themes of partying and having fun would only serve its narcotic purpose for a season, the genre shifted to a glorification of violence and misogyny. Partying and having fun were topics that had a short shelf life in a community that experience longer periods of dismay and despair than they did in revelry. The changing tide of recreational drug use and trafficking of these drugs as well as the lucrative incomes that could be gained in this illegal business sparked a rise in the all ready violent existence of these communities. Party rhymes were increasingly replaced with machine-gun toting rap lyrics about drug selling, and using as well as the financial gain that could be obtained from being involved in it. Consequently, the more edgy the lyrics were the more appealing to the common conscience of violence and outright defiance of societal mores and therefore the evolution of a culture bent on rebellion.

I believe that Hip Hop, the movement, in its marketing, production and consumption became a tool by which rebellion among youth moved from the streets of New York City, Los Angeles, Detroit, Boston and Chicago to the farmyards of Idaho, and the suburban

## The Dusk of Mankind and the Dawn of the Kingdom

sprawls of Sacramento Valley and beyond. American youth regardless of race, color, creed or ethnic origin have embraced the Hip Hop culture. Hip Hop derived themes mark the chosen style of dress that is targeted to the pre-teen and teenage consumer. The blockbuster movie and television industry is also cashing in on this rebellion by including the common thread of a hip hop authenticated main character or plot. The language used by young people across America is reflective of the pervasive influence of this genre of music. Rebellion without a cause bears the face of Hip Hop among American youth.

Of course, Hip Hop is not completely to blame but it is among the culprits responsible for the widespread sense of the hard around the edges rebellion that the MTV generation is portraying as they grow into adults. Hip Hop by no means is the only detracting and influential element of the youth culture because to say that would be to turn a blind eye to other forms of expression that ironically had the same start. Heavy Metal, gothic and hard rock are other genres of music primarily targeting the younger generation and designed to cogitate against what the wider public deems normal or socially acceptable forms of expression. These forms of music and lifestyle among others have spawned their own cottage industries and subcultures that march to their own drum but many times have the same effect as Hip Hop, which has managed to be more in the public view. Heavy metal, gothic and hard rock have all gotten their share of bad press having been connected to acts of adolescent suicide and even the tragic Columbine High School mass shootings that caused America to take a collective deep breath and take notice of the undercurrent of rebellion and rage that was seething among its young people.

## Hugh J. Harmon

Outside of the music influences there is the general power of the media and big business. In our capitalist, market-driven society, businesses use psychological data concerning consumer loyalty, and interest to perpetuate certain schemes of thought. Media in turn goes into contract with big business to boost the bottom line and in turn work together to cushion each other's profits. Television shows are now openly promoting certain images and messages that were once considered taboo, abnormal and immoral. The entertainment industry is subtly and subliminally attempting to redefine morality purging it of all vestiges of its Judeo-Christian background. These messages are pumped into our living rooms daily, and are packaged as family oriented entertainment and defended as being inclusive, open-minded and politically correct presentations of American life.

Our youth lap up these images and are then left to formulate their own ideas of truth. The former counter balance of an adult generation that stood for traditional values and mores, no longer exists. This is because much of the adult population of today is made up of the baby boomer generation that dabbled in the free-love Woodstock experiment if they were of the upper middle class sect, were the actual pioneers of Hip Hop if they were of the lower income urban social status or they were the creators of the Hollywood era-the entertainment media founders and supporters. They have actually grown up but their ideals are still the same. The cultural waves that once were accepted as phases to be dealt with in the industrialization of a nation have become ways of life.

Television, radio, and the internet all former crazes and some were even luxuries have become ways of life for many Americans young and old, poor and rich. Primetime television and radio has become a lineup of inappropriate programming that pushes the boundaries of free speech and expression. Some Americans cannot live without their coffee, and a morning radio shock jock or the midday soap opera marathon. Others can't live without daily sojourns into the cyber netherworld where they take on new identities and some live absolutely different lives from what they know to be reality. Talk shows have replaced social clubs and church fellowships as places to meet and air issues, and in turn receive sound instruction on what to do differently. Americans today live their lives through the advice of television icons and from the "words of wisdom" within the pages of a glossy tabloid or beauty magazine. These form of media have become the modern day pulpits and bibles of truth, respectively.

But theirs is a truth that is at arm's length from Godly derived truth. The Bible says that there is a way that seems tight unto a man but the end thereof leads to death. The scriptures also declare that all of man's righteousness is as filthy rags. Even our idea of righteousness, if it is not derived from God's imputation of righteousness upon us, is nothing but a vain attempt at being right.

As we do our part as believers to cause the kingdom of God to be manifested in our world, the rebellion without a cause of our youth must be reversed. We are dealing with a generation that has grown tolerant of the old time remedies. Tough love no longer has the influence it once had in turning the hearts of young people back to the way of truth. They are living within a completely different paradigm to the generations of old. What they are exposed to as young boys and girls far exceeds even what some generations previously encountered as adults. Due to this paradigm shift and the prevalence of a collective mindset that is unconvinced of traditional views of faith, the kingdom believer must not only teach and talk about the power of God to transform, this generation must see and experience the power of God at work first hand.

Young people need to be convinced that there is a God that transcends the gods of popularity, wealth and the latest trend or fad. They must be convinced that they are better than the loftiest images that cable television chooses to present as reality based television. They have got to be shaken out of the brainwashing experience of addictive marketing campaigns. This is the generation that society repeatedly shakes its head at and declares unchangeable. But this is the very generation whose unwavering spirit and zeal, if channeled heavenward, would passionately change the world. We can't forget the youth and count them out as unreachable because the kingdom movement is in essence itself a youthful movement that thrives on the energetic enthusiasm and childlike zeal of the new faithful.

If we effectively challenge young people to use their natural endowments of energy and drive we can cause a spiritual revolution. A rebellion with a cause can be birthed among young people the likes that this world has never seen before. The young men and women of our society have a key character trait about them that makes them a formidable collective threat to the enemy. This character trait is their loyalty and commitment to things that they feel astutely tied.

One of the greatest strongholds for young people is the dark culture of criminal gangs. The criminal gangs that have our urban and even some of our suburban and rural communities under siege thrive on

# The Dusk of Mankind and the Dawn of the Kingdom

the concept of loyalty. This loyalty is forged in fear and manipulation. The communities in which these gangs exist almost as a cottage industry feeding the criminal justice system, acts as hotbeds for unrest. A character of fear and intimidation marks the general sentiment of the people who live in these communities.

Growing up in this environment young people surrendered to self-preservation, and socialized into fear, find solace in making what the larger society sees as dangerous alliances. Again, the paradigms are quite different for the adult looking in and interpreting the challenges, and the young person on the inside experiencing the challenges. Loyalty is a survival tactic under these circumstances and telling a child to just say no when it comes to gang involvement, and expecting them to make secure choices may sound easier than it is in reality. For many young people the fear of immediate personal injury and ridicule will always overrule fears of spiritual damnation. In other words preaching to at-risk youth about the hell-sending aspect of gang life is something that is of little concern to them in comparison to the likelihood of facing retribution at the hands of thugs in the neighborhood. Spiritual matters are of limited concern to those who lack a sense of physical security.

How do we counteract the culture of misplaced rebellion? The Bible adjures parents to train up a child in the way that they should go. Unfortunately, our society has reinterpreted that text and seems bent on training up children in the way that they would like to go. Too much is left up to the discretion of youthfulness. This is a mistake because young people will always choose the path of least moral resistance. The depletion of the standard two-parent family has contributed to the lack of young people solidly equipped to walk the straight and narrow path. Counteracting the destructive youth culture begins with addressing the issues that are rooted in disjointed and sometimes dysfunctional family dynamics. Churches with a kingdom agenda should have social programming and ministries in place that are dedicated to filling in the gaps of the non-traditional family. Men's ministries should be integrally involved in mentoring at-risk youth. Women's ministries should be doing character and career development activities with the at-risk young ladies. Networks of assistance should be put in place for single parents. These networks should focus on educating the often time young, inexperienced, single mother on the things that they should be focused on fulfilling in the lives of their children.

The issues that face a single mother or a single father for that matter are immense. They range from maintaining employment, child-care expenses, meeting familial objectives, affordable healthcare, keeping up with their child's education and even the possibility of pursuing new relationships. These are all areas that kingdom-minded ministry must attempt to overcome.

Our churches are filled with testimonies of mothers who are both struggling and successful in raising kids on their own. There are examples of mothers unsuccessfully seeking child support. There are even fathers and mothers who've deserted their kids for various reasons. Restoration and reconciliation is required for these individuals too, or else our ministries are doing nothing more than dusting off the issues while not doing anything to eradicate them. We should move from just mere sermons that are indictments of familial abandonment, and reminders to single parents of how they are missing the mark to the establishment of programs that give practical assistance, advice and instruction on raising, maintaining and restoring the family. It's a tough job but somebody has to do it. Broken families will probably always exist in this world but within the church these men; women and children deserve a place of retreat and restoration in Christ.

Gangs are a natural offshoot of the dysfunctional family dynamic. They become the surrogate family for psychologically as well as physically orphaned and abandoned young people. Its hierarchy creates a structure of authority and consistency that many of these kids are crying out for at home. The military once served as the avenue by which this structure and consistency was inculcated into young people who lacked direction, discipline and focus, but unfortunately the criminal gang power structure has taken the lead in this task of acculturating at-risk youngsters into destructive lifestyles of violence. Camaraderie in the gangs, and the restrictive rituals undertaken to gain membership creates not only a sense of family but also delineates identity. The things that gangs offer young people although destructive in their ends are concrete supplements to the things that they need and are failing to receive in their own families, if they have any at all.

Our young people are seeking strong family bonds, forceful leadership that challenges, significance in their endeavors and they need to know that others are taking notice (they strive for acknowledgment of achievements.) These are all concepts that gang life provides to the young person growing up in less than ideal family conditions.

Another way that the church can get into the act of transforming the culture of young people in our society is for the church to expropriate the symbols and images of our youth culture that the devil has managed to pervert. The music of our young people has been co-opted by a culture bent on negativity. Evil has an undue influence on the music, and that influence must be neutralized at all costs. Regardless of what we may believe or think, young people march to a different drum. In fact, we may have marched to sheepskin drums but today they are marching to a drum machine. Old school hymns and choral music may have ministered to us in our loneliest times but it does not have the same impact with young people. We have to look long and hard at ways that young people deeply entrenched in the Hip Hop movement, or the heavy metal craze, or the gothic music scene can be turned onto Jesus Christ. Then we need to look at ways that we can then use these new converts to win their peers to the kingdom.

Some progress is being made in the Christian music arena to attract a younger audience. This is indicative of the increasing number of contemporary gospel hip hop recording artist gaining main stream appeal, as well as the thriving market of Christian rock and pop artist that have in a very short period of time cornered the market on music with lyrical content that is both reminiscent of worship and praise. However, even this progress is dampened when careful examination of the music scene would show some artists although presenting the gospel still presenting it in a way that carries the trappings of worldliness. This is illustrated in the alternative images of some of the Christian rock groups bedecked in tattoos and piercings, as well as the Hip Hop gospel artist that insists on portraying a pants sagging, gangsta-leaning, church thug image. This behavior leaves a lot to be desired and can actually backfire for the church. It just means that more education is needed.

# The Dusk of Mankind and the Dawn of the Kingdom

Young people gifted with the skill to compose witty rhymes that get to the heart of the issues of salvation, redemption and forgiveness should not settle for the status quo. They should not be led to believe that the only way to do Hip Hop or any other musical genre or way of expression is to promote negativity. If we want to make an impact we've got to forcefully redefine the art form. The devil did not create music; all he did was manipulate its practitioners for his own ends. He's not a creator; he's a destroyer by his very nature. Music was his specialty in heaven. What a victory we would have if we were to take back music from the devil? To reclaim our young person we've got to reclaim everything that attracts them, then purify it and sanctify it unto the Lord. This kingdom battle is not designed to win everyone but it is designed for us to get an advantage. God wants us to have an advantage in this life, over evil. Right now sin has an advantage. Kingdom youth, saved, sanctified and Holy Ghost filled are in the minority and that is because the kingdom lost much ground after the fall. Nevertheless, this is the generation that will make up that ground and usher in the final return of the master to set things into ultimate divine order. Kingdom restoration is about wresting control from the grip of the enemy, setting the stage for Christ's return and reconciling all that was God's back unto Him and His authority as the King of the Heavens and the Earth.

## *Kingdom Keys* **for rebellious youth**

The first fact that must be addressed is the generational difference that exists between those who educate, mentor and deal with youth on a daily basis. We must approach this group of young people with an eye for the perspective from which they come and the new paradigm from which they operate. The issues that we dealt with as young people in a world going through transition is quite distinct from what the present generation of pre-teens and teens are dealing with. Our crises stemmed from the pull of youthful rebellion against the status quo as well, but our avenues of rebellion were quite limited. Access to certain material and knowledge deemed adult-oriented was secure from public consumption and therefore children were less likely to ever partake of what we would consider today offensive material. However, with the advent of computers and the proverbial information superhighway that most young people are savvier at navigating than the average adult rebellion in the youth culture has taken on magnanimous proportions. Summarily, we must educate ourselves about the latest trends. The youth of today have the dubious distinction of growing up in a media indoctrinated society that thrives on being entertained, on getting information and communicating information quickly and on instant gratification. The new trend is to live one's life completely in the public eye. Privacy is now something that must be bargained for and this is largely because of the rise in the prominence of celebrity status. And our youth have completely bought into the idea that their lives can too be someday categorized as one to be celebrated in a big way.

Here it comes, the painful truth, the church-the kingdom minded church that is concerned about being a holistic representation of the glorified Body of Christ must embrace that which concerns the youth. This does not mean that tradition must be set aside or even sacrificed just to appease the consciences of a wired generation but rather, that we should implement avenues by which we reach youth within the context of our traditional Christian value systems. Pastors and other church leaders must think of ways to make their ministries relevant to young people. I could hear the collective sigh and the groans of compromise. However, I am speaking of a concerted drive to literally reinvent church as we know it to be church as they need it. What does that mean? That means that our modes of worship have to be contemporized. Even our evangelistic thrust has to be changed so as to not be a turn off to young people but more of a draw. We have to at times individualize our approach rather than depending on the past methods of blanket evangelism. Church's may have to think about remodeling even their appearance. We have bibles now incorporated into palm size computers but we still have Pastors who believe that the church building must look like a gothic cathedral. If we can modernize the Word of God we can surely put a modern spin to the place where we gather to hear it being exhorted. Modes of presenting the gospel have to adapted to become more attractive to this new generation of untapped believers. I call them untapped believers because many of them are believers who are waiting to be introduced to a palatable Christ because the Christ that has been shared with them is a Christ that resents youth and what they like.

Jesus Christ and the message of the Kingdom has to be presented to young people not only as another source of entertainment but as a way of life. Many of the things that were once carelessly categorized as trends or fads that would soon die out among the youth culture have slowly but surely become ways of life for this segment of society. Again some of these trends obviously cannot be adopted by the church because they can in fact constitute plain and simple sin. However, those trends like that of certain forms of music and artistic expression should be co-opted by the church for the betterment and the advancement of the gospel of the kingdom.

## Hugh J. Harmon

### *Kingdom Strategies* **for rebellious youth**

You've got to be willing to fail. That is the first and most effective principle in dealing with an unfamiliar generation. Your willingness to fail will have a twofold affect it will give you an idea of how out of date your traditional strategies of dealing with youth are and it will give you an opportunity to refocus and reassess what it is about your personal ministry that needs to change. Failure can be the greatest teacher because it forces us out of our comfort zone and urges us to be creative as well as. If we never go deep enough to risk failure we will never be able to impact the most desperately needed young people.

Take the chance of employing young people who you see are committed Christians but still are aware of their peers issues. Oftentimes this may take confronting that hard to deal with young man or woman in your ministry that comes but doesn't really seem to be involved. They make every meeting and if asked to contribute they will but never ever really revealing their true sentiments about an activity. I like to refer to them as the "marginally interested" Christian youth. They are fearful enough of the consequences of sin and God's judgment but not convinced enough about what they have been taught concerning it.

Be willing to change how you do church for the sake of making the worship experience more attractive to the younger generation. This should not include making doctrinal sacrifices but it may mean making doctrinal addendums. For example, allowing the young ladies to wear jeans skirts rather than just dresses, or allowing the young men to wear t-shirts and jeans to service as long as they wear these items appropriately.

# The Dusk of Mankind and the Dawn of the Kingdom

This may also include having service on Friday nights or Saturday evenings to offer an alternative to the nite club or the disco. Make the effort to seek out young people who have been involved in church but may have very unorthodox views of the musical expression that still glorifies God and shares the Gospel.

Last and certainly not least, any effective evangelism thrust directed at reaching young people for Christ should have the strong base of a committee whose sole purpose is educating the church about the concerns of youth and working to meet the concerns head on. This committee should be made up of both young people and adults as well with a focus of melding tradition with contemporary concerns while still meeting the mandate of reaching all people for Christ.

# Hugh J. Harmon

# The Dusk of Mankind and the Dawn of the Kingdom

## Chapter Seven

## Declaring Civil War

*And you, that were sometime alienated and enemies in your mind by wicked works, yet now hath he reconciled*

Colossians 1:21

You've probably heard it said before that the spiritual battlefield is the mind. The greatest battles, and for those of us not inclined to violent behavior, the only battles we wage are the battles that are fought between our will and our conscience. The temptation to blame an outside force for our misery is great but each of us in our own way soon comes to the realization that we inflict the greatest damage on ourselves.

In addition, we are constantly engaged in self-defense due to our own doubts. William Shakespeare, the great British playwright and philosopher in his own right, once made a statement that I believe

# The Dusk of Mankind and the Dawn of the Kingdom

encapsulates the idea that I am trying to communicate. He said that *our doubts are traitors and makes us lose the good we oft might win by fearing to attempt.*

The great aim of the mind in the battle that it engages in with itself is the battle for comfort. Mark Twain said in commenting on this issue that a man cannot be comfortable without his own approval. Again this points back to mankind playing a pivotal role in achieving personal peace. Isn't that what it's all about, finding peace? It's about finding that place of balance in our lives concerning what hurts and what helps. When we seek the kingdom we are setting ourselves up to occupy that place of peace that Jesus alluded to in his many sermons on the kingdom.

It is necessary that we draw a distinction here between man's idea of peace and God's kingdom peace. Peace is often defined as the absence of war or conflict, and to a certain degree that definition is true. However, peace in the kingdom sense takes on an even greater dimension of clarity. It is an experience of feeling complete, being unbroken and missing nothing. The kind of peace of mind that kingdom living brings is the peace that is attached to having a sense of wholeness and fulfillment.

The next level of kingdom development within us, after surviving the ensuing rebellion without a cause is the act of declaring a civil war on your mind. The United Negro College Fund's slogan is, " A mind is a terrible thing to waste." But I would like to take some literary license with that slogan and develop it a bit, to clearly articulate the significance of a transformed mind to kingdom advancement. From the kingdom perspective a mind that is unrestrained, and unchecked by a moral conscience is not only a wasted thing but also one that is dangerously unemployed.

The human mind feeds on thoughts. Thoughts are the fuel that drives the engine of our mind. Aimless thoughts like unregulated fuel may allow your car to continue on its journey but in the long run it does more damage to the engine of the mind than it does help it to travel from place to place. The fact of this undue damage done by errant thought is the root cause of our necessity to declare war on our very thoughts. This war is, however, not designed to destroy your mind but rather is with the purpose of winning it over to the purposes of God.

Abraham Lincoln in addressing his fears about the ensuing civil war between the Union North and the Confederate South expressed the fact that the intent of his declaration of war was not to destroy the United States but rather was an effort to strengthen the now fragile commitment to the common good that the then newly independent colonies had made several years earlier. They had severed the last ties they had to British colonial rule and were advancing forward to new statehood as an independent nation with high ideals concerning liberty, freedom of religion and equal rights of its citizens. The country since then had slipped into the doldrums of involvement in the Atlantic slave trade and the unfair capitulation of men and women from a continent on the other side of the ocean completely without recourse. Lincoln was of the impression that war would shake some sense of reason into the South, and eventually lead to a reunification of the states. The kingdom call for declaring civil war is with the intent of bringing our thoughts under subjection to the thoughts and purposes of the mind of God and in so doing reuniting us with our original Godly purpose.

# The Dusk of Mankind and the Dawn of the Kingdom

Why does the mind always seem to be on the devil's list of targets? It is because the mind is the primary base for the exchange of information that enters our conscience. It is because the mind acts as a rational conduit connecting who we are in the flesh, to who we are in the spirit. As discussed previously we are spirit beings occupying a physical shell of a body, but a body nevertheless that is sensitive to its environment. As living souls we are tripartite in being. We have a spirit, soul and body. And at the core of these three is the mind.

The mind is often defined as a component of the soul, and this is true. But that is a structural distinction. When it comes to practicality and function the mind is the tool with which we navigate our physical environment and the tool by which we apprehend the spiritual realm within which we also live. Without our minds we would be helpless to do the right thing in the natural, and we would be unable to tap into the spiritual. We see this on the occasions when we encounter those diagnosed as insane. Those suffering from insanity are unable to function in the parameters of normalcy both psychologically and spiritually. The mind acts as an anchor that keeps us in the here and now while still contemplating where we were and where we would like to be. If the devil can have your mind, he's won the battle already.

One of the first lessons one must learn in any attempt to develop a kingdom focus is that a transformation must take place in the mind. Due to the fact that we have been long alienated from our spirit man the only evidence we have of its awakening within us is a change in our thought life. Our thoughts are the first litmus test of our spiritual renewal. Specifically, our thoughts concerning who we are, our purpose and destiny in this life are among the basic indicators of a spiritual maturation-taking place in us.

The chapters title says, "Declaring Civil War" and the present participle form of the verb declare suggests that it is a continual assertion. We don't just declare war one time it is an ongoing process of war declaration, fighting, periods of peace and then resumption of war. The Word of God, which is our chief weapon in this civil war, is such that reading it one time could never be enough. It is a living prose that reveals new details and relevant information that you could not recognize before but only after several readings and reflections. Apart from the continual revelatory nature of scripture, there's also the proclivity of the human mind to descend back to the basal thinking reminiscent of our human nature, and therefore a constant reprogramming through the Word is needed.

Instruction and correction are experiences of the mind that mark an inclination toward renewal. The mind that is open to instruction is a mind that isn't afraid of being wrong. A mind that is apt to correction is also a mind that has seen its fair share of battles. We are given insight to the attributes of a renewable mind when we peruse the text of the book of Proverbs.

*He who keeps instruction is in the way of life, but he who refuses correction goes astray.*
Proverbs 10:17

This first scripture example teaches us that there is life in receiving instruction. In fact, it lets us know that we avert death when we bow to wise instruction.

# The Dusk of Mankind and the Dawn of the Kingdom

The human mind leans toward conformity to the things of this world. Our minds relish being entertained, and are obstinate when it comes to education. The difficulty of human education is the fault of the human minds propensity to feel that it knows everything. The great obstacle of true enlightenment through education is that the tendency is toward assumptions of accumulated knowledge.

Classrooms are filled with students who feel that they already know all that there is to know about life, the world and their struggles. Therefore, educational systems amble along almost as archaic beast trying to formulate strategies by which they could unearth this so-called hidden knowledge, or surrender their efforts to simple entertainment. Teachers have to become actors, and coax children into learning something that could ultimately make or break their future aspirations. The great theologian and biblical scholar Paul, the apostle, urged the believers at the Church of Rome to not be conformed to this world. The term used by Paul for world in this exhortation was derived from the Greek term 'cosmos', which when defined refers to the idea of a world system. It's not talking literally about the planet but it is referencing the attitude of the individuals that make up the world-their principles and their beliefs. Paul was not saying that we should be non-conformist to the mechanics of life in the world such as breathing, eating and sleeping but he was talking about the things that were wholly separated from necessity and that constituted the doctrine of the human world view.

He urged the Roman believers to be transformed by the renewing of their mind. He believed in the concept of daily renewal of thought patterns. Every time we gather or obtain new information concerning an issue our aim should be to analyze that information against the rubric of God's established Word. Why must our perspectives be continually changing? They should be changing continually because the will of God for our lives is unfolding. As Gods will unfold, more issues are brought to light. There are parts of us that we learn need changing only when our mind is transformed at God's will. How do we gauge whether our mind transformation is aligned with the will of God? We know when; and if our thoughts of what we would like to do, and on what we have done recently are being obedient to God's instruction concerning you.

*Casting down imaginations, and every high thing that exalts itself against the knowledge of God, and bringing into captivity every thought to the obedience of Christ.*

II Corinthians 10:5

If it is not obedient to God it is an argument and a high thing that stands literally in opposition to the knowledge of God. As we declare civil war on our natural mind we must expect tragic results; death has to take place. Old habits, ideas and even likes have to die in this civil war and then and only then can the reign of God's righteous kingdom be actively introduced into this world. It has to start in the hearts and minds of men and women of God, the war might as well be declared because from our day of birth it is being waged.

Probably the most disconcerting thing about growing up and becoming an independent thinker and doer is the issue of realizing that much of who we are lies in what we think of ourselves. And what we think of ourselves is governed by the way in which we handle our thoughts. These may be thoughts of who we are,

## The Dusk of Mankind and the Dawn of the Kingdom

what others think of us, or simply what we should do next in our lives or with our lives.  Growing up through infancy and adolescence and up even on through our teenage years we get the impression that fulfillment or contentment in life was as a result of physical maturation or development.  Young boys feel that if they just could wait till they got a little taller, stronger, bigger or more hairy then they would really make it happen.  Young girls feel that if they could just will their bodies to assume the adult female posture, or if they could get taller, or skinnier and have longer hair then they would attain contentment in life.  Then they were those of us that got scientific and felt that if we could change our diet, and work out, play sports then we would avert the ugly conditions of pimples and acne, and strong smelling perspiration then we would be able to step into adulthood well acclimated and confident.

What a rude awakening it was as we developed through all of the necessary stages—from wimp to jock and realized that it was how we thought of ourselves on a whole that really determined or really mattered to our basic contentment?  The devil, the enemy of our souls, the chief player in the attempts to demoralize us, knows that physical outlook aside; the real leveler of the playing field is how we think not only of ourselves but primarily of what we're going to do now that we know what we know.  He understands the powerful affect of a suggestion.  He knows that the mind and human thoughts are attracted to suggestion.  An open mind can't help but to place some level of focus on a suggestion, especially if that mind is involved in disinterested activity.

Therefore, the remedy for combating conformity is to focus on that which edifies.  As you endeavor to declare all out war on old thought patterns remember that our new thoughts must also be scrutinized. The intent is what God is concerned about. He's looking at why we think the way we do. Part of our civil war siege must be directed at our dark intentions. When we aim to inflict harm and cause hurt feelings those too are dark intentions.

### *Kingdom Keys* **on Civil War in the mind**

Declaring civil war on our minds depends on us voluntarily surrendering to a Godly spiritual examination. It depends on us giving God room not only to search out the intents of our heart but also to reveal those intents to us. Coming to terms with our dark side can be a spiritually therapeutic experience. The side of us that is most damaging to our psyche is usually the side of us that we have little control over because we refuse to acknowledge its presence. Its strength does not lie in its actual potential to harm us but rather lies in our refusal to face it. Dr. Hawkins in speaking on the power of human wills says that that which is injurious to us loses its capacity to harm when it is brought into the light, and we eventually attract to us that which we emanate. In essence he was saying that our dark will causes us not only to attract negativity but also, at the same time, dupes us into believing that it doesn't exist.

God has given us a godly spiritual examiner in our conscience. We however, often buck the commands of our conscience and we thrust forward in evil activity vested in the inert trust that we have in our will—to not only satisfy but to sustain us if we are wrong. Jesus promised his disciples continually that he would not leave them comfortless or alone. He said that he came and he lived and he died to rise again so that his spirit

# The Dusk of Mankind and the Dawn of the Kingdom

might have free reign in the earth. Jesus' short life, death and resurrection released the third manifestation of who he was to the earth realm and gave God entrance in the earth. The Spirit of God, the Holy Ghost that Comforter that Jesus spoke of is operating in the earth. It is still healing, teaching, delivering and setting free and setting up men, women and children. It's stirring up talents, gifts and imparting dreams into the people of God, those who are available to his presence.

Our conscience is the first area within us that God uses to connect to us. Our conscience is literally the last evidence in an unbelieving, dying soul of the original breath of life that God breathed in the clay that was man and made him a soul. The conscience is the part of our souls that still has divine DNA. Therefore, the Spirit of God taps into the conscience training it how to alert the sinner man that they are heading down the wrong track.

The bible says, Behold I stand at the door and knock, and if any man hear my voice. God is saying my Spirit is knocking at the door called your conscience and if you just take heed and obey you shall be made free. Civil war is waging in each and every one of us but if we change sides and hook up with the Spirit of God we'll win. How do you change sides? Believe in Jesus Christ as your Lord and Savior, be baptized in His name as an outward act of an inward change. In fact, become circumcised in your mind, take on the true circumcision not that which is limited to the foreskin of flesh but that which takes away the sinful foreskin of evil in your heart and receive the Spirit of God on the inside. Do it! I urge you to do it, and your life shall never be the same! It shall be exchanged for the life of Christ. You shall be made the righteousness of God.

## Hugh J. Harmon

It's one thing to know right from wrong. It's another to live after right and not after wrong.

# The Dusk of Mankind and the Dawn of the Kingdom

## Chapter Eight

## Letting Go

*Stand fast therefore in the liberty wherewith Christ hath made us free, and be not entangled again with the yoke of bondage.*

Galatians 5:1

Regardless of if we believe it or not we all at sometime in our lives have held on to something far longer than we needed to. We held onto shattered dreams, ruined relationships, and false promises many times unconsciously and vicariously reliving these pitfalls through our successive new relationships. Humanity young and old seems to have an overwhelming tendency to want to hold onto the "teddy and the blanket" of past issues because these issues for some reason create a sense of comfort. Unfortunately, these issues soon turn into idols and we give them an awkward reverence and deference. It's almost as if we are attempting to develop a character for our very lives.

Some people are so attached to the unmet issues, and the regret-laden experiences of their past that they

## The Dusk of Mankind and the Dawn of the Kingdom

seem to find a pride in recounting to peers the problems that they are facing. Letting go of the past is a real struggle of both the saved and the unsaved. Salvation may free you from the penalty of your past decisions but it regrettably doesn't free you from the memory of it. The scars don't disappear; the voices of the nay Sayers aren't quieted and the thoughts of what could and should've been are ever-present.

In the previous chapter we discussed declaring civil war on the human mind. Letting go and living like you're free is actually an extension of that concept—it is an irrevocable part of the cycle of which declaring war is the first step. Kingdom establishment in the earth realm according to the government of heaven requires that believers let go of the issues that are out of our control and literally live in the freedom of the knowledge that God is in control. As we move from the phase of declaration to the stage of actual battle, we've got to understand the unique strategy of kingdom warfare. Kingdom warfare unlike earthly warfare does not depend on our battle readiness but rather depends on how available we commit ourselves to be, in order for God to war through us.

How do we make ourselves available? First, we must come to an agreement as to what being available really means. To be available from the pure sense of the term's definition is to be freed of constraints and made open to receiving something. That may include freedom to receive instruction, or impartation but it is a freeing of the conscience. It is an active pursuit of Godly direction that is without guile. Many of us claim, or believe that we are available for God's use but we never really open up in the right places. We believe that we make ourselves available simply by confessing our faults. That is commendable, but even among friends confession of faults is a regular thing and is not a great indicator of change.

When we confess our faults to God, or even publicly among believers we are merely coming into verbal agreement with God. However, there's more needed in the way of actual repentance. And this also is not just having or feeling remorseful for some evil act committed but rather involves the conciliatory move of turning away from the practice, or thought, or experience that caused us to falter. That is when we make entrance into availability, and that is because God is now able to lead you away from error and into all truth. But as long as you sit and admit you're wrong but you never make an effort to change then you become a sorry, excuse maker. Anyone can make valid excuses and they may even coalesce with facts but God wants us to commit our ways onto Him and then walk in faith. Facts may accurately describe a situation in human terms but faith is supernatural, and brings truth into the picture. Therefore, feeling sorry but never changing just makes us worse off than when we failed to admit we were wrong. But admission of guilt and deliberately acting to change your position is making oneself available.

God didn't make us and set us loose in this great earth just to see us fail. He doesn't relish seeing us defeated. And when I say defeated I mean living in bondage to the perils of your natural life, and to the currents of change in the world. Humanity, outside of God's influence as a collective is fickle. Sentiments, attitudes and feelings about life, the world and the purpose of our existence vacillates with every nuance of change in the environment be it natural, social or economical. The elements that exert a cyclic effect on the planet literally trigger cyclic attitudes among the

## The Dusk of Mankind and the Dawn of the Kingdom

planet's inhabitants. God made us with the original intent of us living above the elements in a seat of control, similar to his existence. However, one man's decision to concede his control to the devil subsequently cost all men the privilege of that authority. As a result mankind took successive steps and falls down a slippery slope to assume a posture of enslavement to the world.

How can we tell if we are also part of this collective mass of individuals enslaved to the world system? We know that we are in bondage when our feelings, actions and attitudes are dependent upon the changes in and, the proverbial ups and downs of our environment. It is normal, natural and sensible to maintain keen awareness and a compassion and concern for the world around us. However, it should not control how we see our own lives. We've got to become agents of change—the breath of fresh air in a time of trouble, the one that is relaxed even when your outward circumstances match those who are falling apart and by the world's standards should fall apart.

What are the indicators of worldly bondage? When societal acceptance of your stance is of utmost importance to you, you're in bondage to the world. We are called to win the world for Christ rather than for the world to win us for the sake of Christ. What do I mean? God didn't call his disciples to be sold out to the world system as a ploy to win men to him. He didn't call us to compromise in the areas of Christian fundamentalism like the sanctity of life and marriage just to win over men and women who want to justify sin-based decisions. God will not justify your act of abortion regardless of your reasons for choosing it just to win you into the body of believers. He's not going to condone your rebound marriages and infidelity done out of supposed loneliness and ignorance just to win you into the body of Christ.  Setting the kingdom agenda through naturalization of new kingdom citizens will require an acculturation of the new convert into the ideology of God's government.

The generational divide that exists between generation "y" and the baby boomer generation is immense.  The efforts of the latter group to minister salvation and present the gospel of Jesus Christ has either been met with overwhelming obstacles or has gained success at the cost of what I perceive as compromise.  The new politic on the issue is that this new generation must be approached according to their world parameters.  There's the idea that if the preacher isn't using hip hop language or other forms of teenage dialect then the collective adolescent body will not take heed to the message.

Some ministries believe that the way to go is to start dance ministries that would take the new age gospel with contemporary influences in the musical arrangements, and meld that with choreography that mirrors the world (just less risqué).  For those not inclined to hit the dance floor there is the ever-increasing influence of youthful, energetic choirs again presenting the gospel with a contemporary sound.  Other ministries have gone the route of Christian rock and even in some cases heavy metal all in an effort to tap into the diverse taste of the untapped population of young souls.

The ministry activities and efforts to bring this segment of society into the believing body of Christ regardless of if it is drama ministries, spoken-word poetic ministries or the occasional (sometimes met with derision) Christian dance clubs that are popping up in

# The Dusk of Mankind and the Dawn of the Kingdom

our urban communities, as cutting edge as these ministries may seem they've got to make sure that they are not towing the line of compromise. We must make sure that we are not further helping to further secure the chains of our youth's bondage to this world.

The church, the real Holy Spirit led church needs to move from merely entertaining the youngsters that attend our houses of worship and begin to really not only educate but empower them for the inevitable difficult days ahead of the believer living in the last days. The world believes that young people can only be reached if they are first entertained. Just take look at the most recent trends in education, even the ones backed by scientific research. They, for the most part, contend that young people do not appreciate the lecturing type of instruction, and in fact they further contend that young people need to have an interactive approach used in their education. They say that the child learns best through self-discovery, experimentation and manipulation and a great teacher is nothing more than a facilitator who stares the child in the direction that they need to go educationally. The best teachers are touted as those who are able to pinpoint a student's weaknesses, identify their strengths as well and then take that knowledge and barter with the student on ways to apprehend what they don't already know.

Simply entertaining a child so that they may develop an interest in knowing who Jesus Christ is will ultimately be a game in which the child will soon lose interest and develop another interest that better tickles their constantly shifting fancy. Sunday School classes for young people have to move from just being feel good sessions where we make crafts and quote poems with gospel themes and move to practical advice and instruction on who God really is and how He can help them to navigate the vicissitudes of this life. Youth groups have to do more than just airing out seminars and forums about teen issues. We have to confront youth with the harsh realities of immature, self-gratifying decisions. The devil is not playing with our youth and we shouldn't be doing the same. Smiling and smirking about improper relationships and the sexual innuendo that sometimes is reminiscent of many a teenage church youth group must be put into the light of the truth of the scars, wounds and pain that infidelity, and fornication even at a young age can inflict.

The sexual urges that our youth are having as young as ages 10 and below are not just as a result of evolving humanity. It is a reflection of the continually declining moral fabric of this global society. It's not just an American problem because I've had the opportunity to travel throughout the western hemisphere and seen documentaries about teen life in Europe and elsewhere. The issues that young people face here are the same issues faced across the globe and even in nations that traditionally had a character of religious turpitude. Alternative sexual lifestyles in their various diverse expressions have touched just about every continent and as a result young people are faced with the issues and consequently the option to choose these lifestyles as categories into which they could place their feelings. In other words, being gay or bi-sexual are terms that have become so familiar it is no longer unusual to find a young adolescent experiencing some feelings that they are unfamiliar with a therefore self-identifying and designating themselves as gay or any of its many alternatives. This is a problem of societal norms for the most part and not a sexual revolution, as some people may think. I've yet to understand how an adult could

## The Dusk of Mankind and the Dawn of the Kingdom

affirm an adolescent's claim of their sexual orientation when they have not yet even fully concluded the stage of puberty. But this is a regular practice in, if not the rest of the world, America. How must we as the church aimed to disciple the world and wanting to include everyone into the fray of soul seeking remain inclusive but yet still exclusive when it comes to affirming traditional notions of family and lifestyle?

How do we, as believers born and essentially raised as citizens of this world, deeply entrenched in its customs and practices, tied to its beliefs for most of our natural lives, relieve ourselves of these encumbrances for the remainder of our natural lives? It's not easy, as much of salvation isn't. In salvation, we are immediately justified by Jesus' sacrificial death, and subsequent victory over death. However, we don't just stay there. We are moved to sanctification where we purpose in our hearts by the leading of the Holy Spirit to separate ourselves systematically from this world.

How will we be sanctified, essentially separated from our former worldly mindset if we still feel that the only way we can establish a relationship with God is on our own terms? Our own terms will always bare the scent of this world because it's natural to us. But walking with God in righteousness is an exercise in the supernatural. It's the practice of powerful faith in God to do exceeding, abundantly above all that we could ask, think or do for ourselves. Young people entrenched in the cultural ties of the hip-hop movement or the rock movement must be educated about the roots of the movement.

The Bible says that my people perish for the lack of knowledge. Our young people are perishing because they are unaware of the origins of many of things that they embrace as part and parcel of their culture. They must not only be told of the glowing attributes that make these different forms of expression good draws for ministry but they must be taught about the negative influences that characterizes much of the movement as well as the way that sin has driven its history. Too many pastors make broad statements about how we can't use the old methods to attract the youth of today but they fail to explain how using the devil's mechanisms will make a lasting impact on a fallen culture. I'm not calling for culture policing from the pulpits but I'm asking for wisdom in adjudging what's Godly and what isn't. Our youth will always be attracted to the familiar sounds of their peers but that sound must be teamed with a powerful in your face message that denounces the secular nonsense of quick money, fame, fornication and misogyny.

There's no secret that Hip Hop has a relatively sordid past. However, it is commonly understood that the sordid past is not based on the music but rather on the individuals who produce it and the messages that they have chosen to highlight in their compositions. Even with the sordid history aside there are still some very positive Hip Hop artist and elements who have tried to take the music to another level not only content wise but also in the spirit with which it is presented. Needless to say, these people have met with great difficulty when it comes to mainstream acceptance and have often been labeled less than authenticated Hip Hop by those involved in the music.

What does this all mean for the young man or woman that grew up in the feverish years of Hip Hop's evolution onto the American landscape as a genre, lifestyle and form of expression to be reckoned with, and seen as a legitimate market driving tool? How are

# The Dusk of Mankind and the Dawn of the Kingdom

they expected to live outside of the fray and maintain traditional values that are many times ridiculed or marginalized by the culture that they are unavoidably considered a part? The answers lie in the church's overall agenda. Are we seeking simply to win souls for Christ or are we just trying to get large numbers of members into our houses of worship? Do we see success in the burgeoning membership role of youth on fire for Jesus or are we just interested in having many members for members' sake?

When we endeavor to co-opt what was once considered wholly secular, and purify it to the glory of God, we've got to be cognizant of the fact that we don't allow the demonic aspects of the culture to remain evident in the shift just so that we could attract young membership. As I sit and view the occasional Gospel Hip Hop video on Christian television I am sometimes driven to cringe at the presentation because it seems to still drip with the seething attitudes of anger and rage that so characterizes the darker elements of rap music. Apart from the rage there is also the fascination with gaudy portrayals of wealth (i.e. artist dripping with diamond encrusted jewelry and driving expensive cars) There's nothing wrong with letting the world know that in God there's opportunity to live comfortably and to acquire just as much as, or greater than the world is able to accumulate but is that a message we want to continue to propagate. When it comes down to it, the world will always win that battle because in Christ prosperity and favor are tied to the purpose behind the gained wealth. Until a young man or woman is taught that God gives us the power to get wealth so that we can cause His kingdom to come to pass in their life time, and to advance the agenda of spreading His gospel I think their mindset will still be that of having wealth just to flaunt it. And this is something that can be achieved by worldly living.

Being that I am a very analytical person I was always of the impression that the genre of music was dependent upon the common sound. One can tell a country and western song by the sound of the chords and plucked guitar strings and by the musical arrangement even before one hears the lyrics. The same can be said for just about all forms of music including Hip Hop. Therefore, like many other believers who struggled with the concept of putting what we loved by the way of music prior to salvation aside for the dry and often slow dirge of church hymns and such I thought that when it was all said and done the lyrics were what was important. If we were concerned about the Word of God getting out to all men then it should therefore make sense to assume that the lyrics of Gospel music was what mattered. Therefore, when I got saved and I caught the first beats of a Gospel Hip Hop sound and realized that I could still love the music that I always loved and not rescind my salvation I wholeheartedly plugged into the Gospel Hip Hop movement. However, I soon realized that although the general theme of the lyrics was changed to glorifying God, I still heard some rhymes that I now believe are a subtle way of the enemy to invade even that genre and taint its ultimate goal.

What do I mean? For example, I remember in the days when I listened to secular rap and reggae there were certain lines in the music in which the artist made a witty comparison. Those comparisons were what made the music so good. The wit in the rhyme was what made us laugh and get into the groove. On those occasions it wasn't so much that the artist used foul language or said something that rang out as evil and it

# The Dusk of Mankind and the Dawn of the Kingdom

appealed to our soulish side but it was nevertheless entertaining. Then they were artist who took the semantics even farther and instead of just using witty comparisons they integrated into their rhymes, words that replaced those nasty little words that make up our foul language vocabulary. These words and catch phrases inevitably became a part of the culture and were deemed acceptable because they weren't the actual "cuss word" but they referred to them. In some cases these words have crept into the Gospel Hip Hop genre. They might not be referencing an outright use of foul language but they may be espousing the negative lifestyle choices like weed smoking, or drinking of liquor. I have found that some contemporary Christian artist have found ways to on the one hand speak against the activity but yet still on the other hand, glorify it. There's a thin line that is then created between out and out condemnation of a lifestyle, and complacency for it.

As young Christians, with a penchant for rhyming and a love for the beats and rhythms that are part of the appreciation of Hip Hop when you come into salvation and become sold out for Christ one should really consider what matters most. Does it matter more to be authentic and have street credibility as a rapper, or is it to be a Christ transformed purveyor of the good news?

The scriptures teach us that even more significant than the activity is the spirit in which that activity is done. It is a painful experience to witness a young man or woman engaged in some form of Hip Hop or rock music expression labeled as Christian and still portraying the anger, the excessive gyrations and gestures (i.e. the crotch grabbing, the holding of the fingers to the lips like you're smoking) that are solidly part of cultural norms that we need to get them away from.  Those actions, attitudes and gestures aren't okay when used by the secular artist and they must not be considered acceptable when used by the Christian artist.  These distinctions must remain between what is secular and what is sanctified music because without it we're left with the question of whether the aim was performance and entertainment rather than praise and empowerment.

   Even lifestyle must be sanctified.  We've got to encourage our young people to a higher standard than even those considered good people in the world.  Even those practices that seem innocent carry with them an evil origin.  Sometimes our intent of innocence can be overpowered by the origin of evil.  Our intent for getting involved in certain activity may be simply as a result of an urge to have 'harmless' fun but even on those occasions the enemy may be working up a scheme to us into something that appears harmless but is ultimately harmful.

   Let's take tattoos for instance.  I remember I was fascinated by the whole artistry and I just thought that they were a 'cool' way to express my uniqueness.  I wanted to stand out and be different and give off this exotic air.  There were females that thought I was attractive already but I thought that if I just added tattoos to my mystique I would be irresistible.  So you see my minds intent was superficial but my hearts goal was even deeper. Many people are not that deeply entrenched in their decision making when it comes to tattoos but regardless of that fact most of us who do or did get them were simply thinking it was harmless fun.  Outside of the medical concerns or the possible physical side effects I was determined to get at least one experimental tattoo.  Little did I know that this

# The Dusk of Mankind and the Dawn of the Kingdom

harmless act would be the opening of a doorway for evil into my very soul! It sounds spooky and otherworldly but it is true. When I allowed that man to carve those symbols into my flesh and deposit that indelible ink I was also cutting a pathway for evil influences to enter. It wasn't that the literal cuttings of my skin open a gateway in the natural but it was that my infraction of a spiritual command led to the invitation of evil into my sphere of existence. Tattooing is strictly biblically prohibited, and although I was ignorant of this at the time, I still had to suffer the consequences.

*Ye shall not make any cuttings in your flesh for the dead, nor imprint any marks upon you: I am the Lord.*
Leviticus 19:28

Some theologians and pastors even today argue that this was an Old Testament law, and that it was specific to the ancient Hebrew people. They would go on to say that God was trying to teach them that separation from the practices of their heathen enemies would set them apart as a precious people unto Him. Some ministers even counsel their young members who are interested in tattoos that they should get something that is illustrative or symbolic of being a Christian if they do decide to get one. But I believe that the Word of God is clear in saying that not one jot or one tittle shall in no wise pass from the law or fail from the law.

Desiring a tattoo to pay homage to a loved one or to something that you're passionate about, in and of itself is not wrong or evil. However, going through with the desire will consequently be an infraction of God's law and will lead to the imposition of evil upon our lives that we didn't necessarily intend to entertain. I might not intend to invite mosquitoes and flies into my house at night but if I intentionally open the porch screen door to get some fresh air I would be unintentionally inviting those pests in especially if I have the light on. It's the same with some of the things we get involved in, out of wanting to be down with the trends and seeking harmless fun.

The cutting away of the skin to leave scars, tattoos, brands and making other symbolic cosmetic and often-painful adjustments to our physical features in their origins, centuries ago, were part of and still is a part of pagan worship. The markings or symbolisms were often indicative of one's allegiance to a particular deity, or a tribe. We may use the argument that we are purifying the practice by tattooing Christian symbols into our skin but when it is all said and done, are we really glorifying God or are we just fulfilling a fleshly desire to draw attention to ourselves.

I'm writing again as one who has several tattoos and who got them just to be different. I wanted to do something that would set me apart from my peers, something extraordinary. I did some research on tattoos before I got them and even with the information that I had gathered concerning the origins of the practice I still went ahead I got them done. I was blinded by my selfish need to make a statement and to redefine who I was. It is impossible for one to get as involved in tattooing as I have to not become aware of the dark aspects and even the satanic nuances that are reflective of the tattoo subculture on a whole. I still went ahead and dived into it, I know sit here clad with a fire breathing dragon motif, Egyptian pyramid with an all-seeing eye symbol dripping a single tear and several tribal symbols some of which I really do not know the deep meaning connected to them.

# The Dusk of Mankind and the Dawn of the Kingdom

But I thank God for grace, because even though I was unsaved, far from God, and not interested in salvation at the time when I was doing this, he still saw fit to deliver me from what at one time had become an addiction. I wouldn't say that I was shielded from the consequences of my action because I wasn't. I do believe that a large percentage of the satanic influences that I have had to struggle with and still struggle with since those days were as a result of the tattoos that I got. They started out as a fad; something cool to do. They eventually became something that set me apart from my peers, especially those I had branded as "stiff-necked" conservatives, and apart from the intellectual demigods that I had counted myself among. It began as a fashion statement and evolved into an ideological stance upon which I began to build a philosophical rationale. This is what often happens with complacency of subtle evil. We engage in activity be it the kind of music that we listen to, the movies that we watch, the websites and chat rooms that we visit and despite the questionable nature of these activities we move step by step deeper into compromise. We may even begin a bit apprehensively but sooner or later, the devil doesn't really care when, our flesh becomes accommodating and then our minds become accustomed and then our hearts work to rationalize the juxtaposed discomfort and pleasure that it feels. The next thing we do is begin to create a script within which we can dabble in satanic games, believe in a God, but never come to salvation. We could never receive salvation because our apprehension turned accommodation has birthed a customization that has made us immune to the idea of being broken with a need for some fixing.

In order for us to really let go and live like we're free we've got to give up running after the fads. All the latest trends aren't aligned with a godly lifestyle.

Lifestyle speaks of the fashion of one's living. And to be honest much of what the world is doing is really a death-style. They are simply finding more advantageous ways to practice dying. It's as if they're trying out different weapons, or poisons. They're daily trying out new death-causing devices rather than strapping into new life-saving devices. Bondage is death seeking, and freedom in Jesus Christ is life seeking.

    The main thing we have to get out of this teaching is that we not only have to release physical burdens to the Lord but we must also release spiritual burdens to Him as well. I'm weary of preachers and evangelist who degrade or even ironically dismiss the dimension of spiritual renewal. The language used in those cases usually is, "It doesn't take all of that. You're being too spooky, and spiritual binding here, and loosing there." But I would propose in hearty opposition to such suggestions that preaching that neglects spiritual empowerment and significance is no more than motivational speaking that profit but for a season. The spirit realm has equal or even greater influence on our destinies than the natural forecast of our lives. As we are bound by worries and concerns over what we see, we too are bound by external spiritual influences that are dedicated to our ultimate victory or destruction. But God has placed at our disposal keys to access that realm and keys to put those burdens at his altar and reject death. Those keys include primarily that of prayer and that of faith.

    Prayer and walking in and by faith are keys that are acutely tied to submission. Prayer is actually an act of submission to God. When we pray we submit our request to Him and we surrender ourselves as well. Faith in its very nature is not just belief but it is action

# The Dusk of Mankind and the Dawn of the Kingdom

that depends heavily on a divine response. When it comes to faith it appears that we do very little here in the natural and the physical but in the invisible world of the supernatural and the spiritual much is happening.

The very root of resistance to evil is submission. If you are able to submit unto God you will be empowered to resist the enemy. Yielding ourselves unto God is an act of resistance to our selfish nature of wanting and feeling as if it is in control. The scriptures commend us to submit ourselves unto the Lord, when we do then our next step of resistance to the devil will be effective. My freedom and my release depend on my flesh coming under the hand of God.

Kingdom living in a condemned world requires that we live outside of the limitations of ourselves. It's not a reaching within to get a greater self-knowledge, but it's a reaching out to the Spirit of God that He may eventually reside inside of us. My inner strength, and potential are great, and they can cause me to think myself out of a thing that I truly can't get myself out of. But I need the spirit of God to penetrate my person and cause death and resurrection to take place within me. As long as I try to figure life out by myself, I will continue to develop false hope and experience continual failure. Adam and Eve's error in the garden at the beginning of time has pretty much solidified our chances of guaranteed failure in depending on ourselves to save us. But if we surrender, repent and yield our weaknesses, our lack, and ourselves unto Him we shall once again taste victory and success through Jesus Christ.

Adams success before the fall was due to his submission to the ruler-ship, mandate and authority of

God in fulfilling God's purposes in the earth.  Every bit of the first man's success was because God led, God controlled and God obtained as a result of his actions.  If we desire success, peace, fulfillment and comfort we must let God lead, control and obtain all that he has set to obtain through us.  In other words, my peace is wrapped in God's purpose.

Many of us believe that peace is in searching out, and seeking after things that will satisfy our senses, and our feelings.  And unfortunately we've realized, often after being hurt over and over again, that our senses and our feelings can never be satisfied; they're insatiable.  The gut of my senses, and my feelings can't be filled.  Think about it, our eyes seek after beauty when pursuing intimate relationships and maybe for a season that person's beauty may captivate us.  However, if our attraction remains merely sensory, and our feelings stay sensual our eyes will soon wander in an effort to pursue satisfaction in something new.  Many times new does not necessarily mean better, it's just that our soulish desires require constant change.

Our eyes should never be the tools by which we gauge our fulfillment in life.  The food that is most pleasing to the physical palate is often that which is most detrimental to our physical health, especially if indulged in excess.  This again shows that sensory satisfaction is a fleeting experience, but spiritual fulfillment is possible, in fact, it's one decision away.

Our life is a spiritual journey as much as it is a litany of physical and psychological moves and stops.  Daily in the natural world, we walk at the mercy of physical incidents and accidents much of which we are able to see and avoid.  In the supernatural, however, we are at the mercy of spiritual assault, but God's grace

# The Dusk of Mankind and the Dawn of the Kingdom

covers what we cannot see. Lord help us to remember that each day we make it through it's because you've granted us the privilege, you protected us from a fiery dart and you shielded us from another demonic accident waiting in the wings. Therefore, we relish in the fact that physical freedom is good but even more importantly spiritual freedom in Christ is the greatest, so we're going to let go and live like we're free.

### *Kingdom Keys* **on Living Like You're Free**

The primary key is submission, and more succinctly surrender. These two words or actions are probably some of the most resented words in Christendom. But without them the work of Christianity is incomplete. Letting go and living like we are free citizens in God's kingdom will require us to walk according to the guiding principles of God's kingdom. That means we must submit to this rule and surrender to His innate law. It is an innate law because it is implicitly expected when His Spirit dwells within us and there is no need for a written code to live by.

All of our lives we've been living as we pleased. We've been subject to the law of our flesh. In fact, we were faithful servants to it. It's natural for the physical body to serve the laws of nature. But what are the laws of our nature? Human nature can be defined as the essential character, disposition or temperament of a person. Nature is derived from the Latin root word natura (nasci) that refers to being born as. When we are doing things according to our nature we are acting without affectation, pretense or inhibitions we just simply doing what comes normally to the flesh.

Due to this understanding of human nature it becomes clear that in order for us to live a transformed life a fundamental core value change has to take place in us.  This change in core values is necessary because too much of what we are, and what we have become as people separated from God is so engrained in us that even when Jesus creates the loophole of salvation for us to escape, and giving us a new nature we unconsciously resuscitate the former nature.  We believe that the way we used to live, is the only way to live.

   Most of us prop back up the corpse of our former selves somewhere in the closet of our minds just to revisit him or her occasionally for advice and instruction on tackling old issues.  We were unsuccessful in our methods of approaching these old issues or habits but yet still we depend on that failed methodology for answers.  That is a sign of insanity.  The old nature of sin is literally deranged and "out of its' own mind".  The old man dies at the cross but we act like God and try to put life back into it.

What are the characteristics of the human nature?
- Self-preservation
- Self-knowledge
- Self-benefit

That means that it is essentially selfish, and to be selfless as the kingdom requires would be an unnatural state of being for the human nature.  Without the supportive framework of God's spiritual guidance and faced with a choice we would always choose that which will bring us greater individual benefit.  In our eyes if we can calculate a beneficial outcome that makes us feel, seem or appear better that is the one we would choose naturally.

   We lie simply because in some way it makes us feel better in ourselves, seem better in our actions and appear better to our peers.  Lies are a way in which we

# The Dusk of Mankind and the Dawn of the Kingdom

construct a false character, and therefore satisfy the ego's need to be admired. We cheat, again in an effort to make our old self-happy. Shortcuts, and breaking the rules are always good choices to the human nature once they lead to the desired end. It's human nature to be jealous or envious of others because we see the other person having some advantage over us either in possessions or perception.

That means that human nature is both divisive and dangerous. As long as we hold on to what we used to be outside of salvation and outside of our new kingdom affiliation we will continue to march with a disposition that is headed to destruction. Every aspect of our fallen nature is literally driven towards decay.

How do we escape this successive progression to death? First, we've got to accept the truth of our condition and then we've got to let God change our nature. The new birth is the acceptance of a new nature. We are being recreated in Christ to be a reflection of another aspect of Him. How do we do this? We do it by faith in Jesus Christ to do what he said he could and would do for us.

Taking on a new nature begins with acting in faith. Our new nature is not visible or perceptible to the naked eye and therefore has to be spiritually discerned. We can't depend on the world to stoke the embers of our new nature because it doesn't respond to man's cheerleading. It only responds to God. Lying, cheating and stealing and all other strategies that we once used to make ourselves feel better about ourselves will no longer work to convince us that we are wonderful. In fact, they'll sooner convict us that we're wrong when we take on Jesus Christ's nature.

The Bible says by faith, through grace we are saved and not by works less any man boast. We see here the significance of faith. It takes us out of the dimension of boastful intent. It takes us out of doing things for a handclap, pat on the back or kind words. When you operate in faith you're doing what you do to satisfy God's purpose. And that purpose is not just for you to gain spiritual stripes, or applause from Him but is simply that He might get the glory. This is where true freedom dwells. When you do things, say things, or even think things that are completely out of a sense of wonder at God's plan for the world, and without a thought of how your own little world will be compensated.

# The Dusk of Mankind and the Dawn of the Kingdom

## Chapter Nine

## The Great Challenge

*He who believes in Me, the works that I do he will do also; and greater works than these he will do, because I go to My Father.*

John 14:12

What is the great challenge of this life? The great challenge of this life is for us to believe God. It might sound simple just to believe, but by all appearances it isn't as easy as it may seem. Belief depends on the individual ascending to a position of acceptance of a thing or a concept without necessarily having a full understanding of that concept. This nebulous nature of belief is what makes it difficult to ascertain. This is why most of the world still finds it a great feat to believe in much of what confessing Christians confess as the truth.

For us to believe God wholeheartedly we have to confidently trust that what we know about Him is true. We live our lives by truth, and belief is the avenue by which we access and process what we understand to be the truth. Every one of us walks, acts and even thinks according to a set of truths that we hold to be valid defining concepts about the world around us. Our understanding of how money works, of the processes of law and even of our own biological makeup is based on our accumulated knowledge of the world, and that knowledge for most of us delineates our truth.

The problem with the world is that one half of us are living according to a set of 'truths' that really constitute a lie, and the rest of us are living according to *the truth*. The newly converted believer finds him or herself in a quandary to renovate their thinking so that it aligns with the mind of God, and resists going back to formulating understanding based on worldly 'truths' which are really masqueraded lies. These are realities that the unbelieving world finds difficult and I daresay, even offensive.

It offends the common man to think that all of his life's assumptions to this point concerning his purpose or lack thereof are erroneous. This continues to be the stumbling block that hinders true revival in this age. It offends people to think that there might be a single way to abundant, peaceful and joy-filled lives. And it is especially offensive when they consider that this single way to truth is via belief in a God that condescends to give his life that we might have life.

Human understanding of God outside of the Christian worldview paints a portrait of an impersonal super-being that really has no use of humanity. To many, God is just another being that can't be trusted because we've been indoctrinated to not trust anything that is more powerful than us. The vastness of which is God-the indescribable everything that He is causes mankind to define Him out of our own understanding.

God's omnipotent greatness and His unreachable wisdom create a paradox from which we are unable to define Him and His will without offending our own person.

Nevertheless, God calls us to believe Him at all cost. We've got to believe that He did what He did, and said what He said without ever being able to truly prove it outside of simply believing. There's nothing that Jesus asks his disciples to do more of. Belief was the constant bridge across which Jesus beckoned the lame and the sick to come for healing, and the sinner to come for salvation.

Why is belief so important a step for us to take in approaching God, and in establishing his kingdom here? It's because belief in and of itself, contains the intangible quality of acceptance and trust that does not depend on understanding. This quality is what makes it that much more appealing to God as a mechanism by which he could validate the depth of our relationship with Him. We can't understand God regardless of how hard we try but we can accept his judgment.

It would've been easy for God to make humans with an inability to choose outside of Him. However, that would not have been a loving arrangement. Love must be based on choice and on acts of free will. If He had made us with a captive will we would've been obedient simply because we didn't have the power or the capacity to do otherwise. Therefore, belief had to and still has to be a part of any lasting relationship between God and man. Our love for Him more than our fear of Him must be based on what we believe about Him.

# The Dusk of Mankind and the Dawn of the Kingdom

The apostle Paul says in his second epistle to the church at Thessalonica, that we are bound to give thanks always to God for you, brethren beloved of the Lord, because God hath from the beginning chosen you to salvation through sanctification of the Spirit, and belief of the truth. That's a powerful statement by the apostle on the significance of belief in our ability to be saved. Belief was selected as a guiding principle in the original plan of God to win man back to Him.

The devil knows how powerful belief could be. His very aim in every attack is to birth in us a spirit of unbelief and doubt. He comes but to steal, kill and destroy through doubt. It's the method he used in orchestrating the original sin. He caused first Eve and then Adam to doubt God's intention toward them. The moment they doubted God they metaphorically fastened the shackles of death upon their spirits. They committed spiritual suicide, and removed themselves from spiritual contact with God. This is why God asked the question of Adam, "Where art thou?" He sensed that Adam no longer existed in the dimension of spiritual sensitivity. To remain free from the bondage to death all Adam had to do was to believe what God had said, and rebuke his wife's offer, and ultimately the devil's suggestion that God was lying.

The devil's strategy in constricting our ability to believe God is threefold. First, he introduces doubt. He takes what God said and offers an alternative philosophical interpretation of God's intent. Often times God's intent is clear and the devil knows that but he also knows that we are rational beings always trying to think things over. Secondly, he encourages the pursuit of knowledge. Knowledge becomes paramount in our minds and we hinge our belief on what knowledge we have of a thing. This is a dangerous ground on which to walk because our knowledge will always fall short of explaining the all that God is and can do. Last and certainly not least is the third stage of demonic strategy and that is possession. This is when he convinces us that virtue and truth are of no particular significance to your existence and that those are tools of the weak and insecure. This is when the devil has taken possession of your person. Evil becomes no longer intolerable but rather becomes an inviting alternative to a boring virtuous life. We start acting like this when we are far removed from believing God to change our situation. Debauchery always seems more tacitly appropriate the less and less we feel about our ability to change.

The Bible declares that Abraham even while standing in a place of hopelessness from a natural perspective believed God to give him a son, and from that son a generation that would be called blessed. And the declaration concludes on this wise, and he counted it to him for righteousness. Abraham's justification as proclaimed in the book of Romans was not due to any outward action on his part but primarily was based on his belief-the inward action of his heart. To believe God is to turn our affections, and our trust toward God and that demands a turning of the heart.

The great challenge is in believing that all it takes is belief. We are so accustomed to critically questioning the levels of trust that we can put in others, we most of the time live our lives unable to believe without concrete evidence. Belief seems too trivial a way to solve the problems that we face. This is because our understanding of belief is limited to that which we are able to see. Hence, we have the widely accepted statement that seeing is believing.

# The Dusk of Mankind and the Dawn of the Kingdom

Belief is a life-preserving attribute. In the biblical Genesis account of the great flood, Noah secured the preservation of himself and his family because he believed what God said. Imagine his position, standing confident and following God's direction for years when the public sentiment of his day was a complete rejection of God. The men of Noah's day were marching further and further into apostasy and it was partly because of them understanding how powerful they were. They were giants, the bible describes them as mighty men of old but it also says that their wickedness was great and every imagination of their hearts was evil. But Noah found grace in the eyes of God.

Evil literally became a pastime for mankind. He did not just do evil things out of ignorance they deliberately and designedly practiced it, while continually contriving new ways to do it. But Noah even in the midst of such carnage believed God. It takes a special anointing to do right in the face of, and while standing in the midst of exceptionally accepted evil. Everyone else was doing it. There was no one that reflected a moral compass upon which humanity could fix their eyes and therefore pull them out of the miry clay of sin.

The American south during the slave era and the early Jim Crow years of civil rights unrest and reform was similar. The exceptionally accepted evil was human enslavement and discrimination. Southern land owning whites saw their treatment of these American descendants of Africans forcefully brought to this land as an acceptable practice necessary for the maintenance of their plantocracy. Even after slavery one would be hard pressed to find a Southern white resident who thought that segregating blacks to the deplorable existence of sharecropping and underserved schools and communities was wrong. They actually saw it as giving them a fair shake. I wonder how many people who lived during that time whites or blacks truly believed that some day it would all change.

Nazi Germany was under a similar condition. The spewing of hate speech targeted at those considered the minority in the Germanic world at the time, primarily Jews, got widespread acceptance by the German populace and in some cases much of Europe. The argument was that these Jews had come into Eastern Europe and had artfully managed to monopolize the best jobs, property and businesses. Hitler created a veritable cottage industry of distrust for Jews branding them as opportunist that used their wealth to take what was rightfully the possession of the original people of the German hinterlands. This kind of warped retelling of history created a tension among poor Germans that led to a deliberate retaliation against Jews that eventually led to holocaust and the Nazi contemplations about the final solution of annihilating an entire ethnicity of people. When we view film clips even today of the German oppression of Jews and their exiling them to ghettos and concentration camps one can hardly find any public outcry among the German society. The activity of Nazism had so been ingrained into the public conscience. What would the Jews have given for a voice or a heart that believed in justice during those evil days?

The great challenge for us today is to have a Noahic resolve. It's to start working, constructing the things of the kingdom at God's leading while having no evidence of his impending return. It is do the things of God, serve, preach, teach and love others all while having no tangible evidence beyond a heartfelt belief that He is, and will reward your work in due time. It is

# The Dusk of Mankind and the Dawn of the Kingdom

dealing with the derisive naysayers and those subjecting you to ridicule for your stance while still believing God. To believe is to fear. Noah feared God more than he feared the derision of men.

Who do you fear more? Do you fear the comments and criticisms of those who consider your faith more like folly? At work, do you opt out of identifying yourself as a Christian because you believe in some way by not saying it you won't offend the sensibilities of those who don't believe? When others point fingers and accuse all Christians of being hypocrites, do you nod in agreement? It's challenging to be the lone dissenter but that's what God is looking for from you.

There will come a time in your life when you will be thrust into a situation in which you will be challenged to stand for righteousness simply because of what God told you. It won't depend on what you see, or on what you feel but entirely on an intangible Word that was spoken to you sometime prior. God seldom challenges us to respond immediately to a Word. He most often includes the dimension of patience to prove the level of our faith. As we try to cope with the challenge of belief we've got to understand that a Godly stance is seldom a popular position to hold. There will be more people against you in the natural than they are for you. We've also got to understand that the devil will never make it look better, sound better or feel better than we would like it.

The ancient Hebrew nation, at one time a small group of men and women descended from a common relative Abraham had to be a people of belief. Despite Abraham's personal blessings the nation that he produced by the providence of God had to believe in

God even when it appeared that the promise made to their forefather and repeated to them as children contradicted all reality. How could this band of twelve socially maladjusted brothers of a blended family, with issues of jealousy among them, possibly be the generational seed from which God himself would birth his plan of redemption for all mankind? It was belief that kept Joseph, one of these twelve in his right mind even after being sold into slavery by his brothers. Can you believe God like Joseph did? Would you still stand on his Word if you found yourself laying on your back in a pit for no apparent reason? Would you still feel a need to depend on Him if you dwelt in a palace? This is the profound example we need to take heed to, because success many times causes us to come down from our standards, and opt out of belief because we have money or prestige. Why should you believe in God even if you have it all? You should because His hand is what's keeping what you have in your possession. It's His amazing grace that's keeping you above the red of bankruptcy. It's His will that has given you a passport to prosperity, and it could be His will to redeposit that favor with someone else.

The great challenge is to believe like Moses that even with his stuttering speech and fearfulness he could confront God's enemy in Egypt. The challenge is to believe beyond our limitations that God is able to impute upon us his unlimited power to rule over the circumstances of our lives. It was this kind of kingdom-minded belief that caused Joshua to boldly press forward, and proclaim, "As for me and my house we shall serve the Lord." Do you have an "as for me" spirit concerning believing God?

Living in a world of contradictions, where every principle and philosophy birthed in the minds of men is toward elevating their own ability; it is difficult to submit to God through mere belief in His ability. A world driven by independence, and the pursuit of it, lacks the initiative to believe in anything outside of itself. We are taught in our school systems to believe in ourselves. Our motto has become I can do all things through my own strength, intellect and influence. While the Word of God says, I can do all things through Christ who strengthens me.

If it is difficult for you to believe what you cannot see, calculate or estimate then you will soon realize that your mathematics will never solve the problems of your life. You may come to an answer by adding some figures here, and subtracting some figures there, but your total will always come short of what you need. Believing in your paycheck, and your retirement funds is a serious mistake that we make as we contend to make life easier for ourselves and our family. These things may offer a level of comfort but they will never bring contentment. Comfort is an external experience but contentment is an internal disposition. Money will never be able to bring us contentment because it lacks the ability to preserve us if the collateral we possess loses its value. When the stock market crashed several years ago, we had a nation of investors with humungous paychecks and attractive retirement packages on paper who immediately went from comfort to crisis. The collateral that they had accumulated over the years had now become worthless with one momentary slip in the mindset of the market.

The great challenge is to take our eyes off of our weaknesses, and inabilities, and see that every conflict does not require our fight. We've got to choose which issues are battles and which are wars. Life is strewn with many battles but we are ultimately engaged and enlisted as soldiers in one war. The Bible says, "For though we walk in the flesh, we do not war after the flesh." There's one spiritual war but many physical battles between us, others and our own flesh. Maintaining the kind of perspective that says that the negatives that we go through in the physical cannot and should not be compared to what God desires to do positively for us in the spirit is necessary. We may wake up each morning and see despair, and be tempted to give up hope but the fact that we have endured yet another day is evidence enough that something great is taking place inside of us. God sometimes causes the externals of our lives to remain unchanged so that he might force us to take account of the spirit. Nothing will change for the better in our lives if we do not engage the spiritual side of ourselves.

We engage our spiritual selves through the disciplines of the spirit. Prayer is a spiritual discipline that we have access to, and one that desires very little experience for one to make a regular part of their life. Daily we must embark on the spiritual discipline of communicating with God. Too many of us pursue prayer only when we're in dire straits and all other avenues of relief had been exhausted. We come to God in prayer as a last resort when a family member or we ourselves are on death's bed. We begin to pray when in our perspective, all is lost or all other avenues have been exhausted. It should be the other way around. Prayer should precede every endeavor. We should be most earnest in prayer when we have it all. Our prayer should be one not only of thanksgiving but also of direction. We many times make plans with our money and our lives and only after we notice issues of concern developing with our plans then we go to God in prayer about a backup plan. Part of our great challenge is to pattern our lives according to the Godly response we get

## The Dusk of Mankind and the Dawn of the Kingdom

in our prayers; rather than patterning our prayers according to the outcomes of our lives. Prayer should be a precursor of problems because it will give us the strength necessary to overcome unavoidable issues that develop in a world corrupted by sin.

We've got to understand that problems are going to come our way, some major and some minor. Prayer should never be relegated to knee-jerk reactionary status in our lives. It should be a consistent practice that will resultantly equip us with the resolve to see the problems to their conclusion. Prayer brings spiritual clarity to the confusing conflicts of this world because it entertains a divine response from the one who is keenly aware of the deepest dimensions of our issues. The problems we face in life are often packed with many layers that we ourselves are unaware of. We are only privy to how it makes us feel at that moment or to how it may be affecting our level of comfort. But there may be several people affected or even benefiting from your season of difficulty. This ultimately must be the perspective that we maintain as we endeavor to do our part to express the kingdom in this world. Prayer opens our understanding to these different dimensions and gives us the sense of perfect peace even in the midst of an evident storm in our lives.

If we were to take the irony of the Hurricane Katrina tragedy and dissect just a portion of the dilemma we can see the need for a spiritual mindset. It was clear the devastation that this natural disaster wreaked upon the levies and consequently upon the livelihoods of the citizens of that region. However, did you ever consider the kingdom-minded believers who lived in the area that was directly hit, the ones who not only lost homes but lost family members in the ensuing floods. Think about it, praying folk, believing folk and unbelieving folk were displaced. Tears were shed, rage was expressed, and blame was directed at the city officials, state government, etc. Could the devastation really be avoided? If we took a really hard look at what happened it was clear that this natural disaster could not be prevented. Nevertheless, public sentiment drove Americans to seek someone to blame. A kingdom-minded perspective would have us to see that despite the deaths and the economic destitution, the forced relocation that occurred after rescue missions began may have been a welcome change for some of these residents. Finally, the nation and the federal government would take notice of the plight of the jobless, poverty-stricken and crime-ridden environment of the Eighth Ward. Maybe now the political establishment could be held to their promises and real change in the social strata of the New Orleans underclass will take place. After the flood maybe now money will be infused into the economy of the region. Maybe now development would take place in communities that had no future of coming out of the doldrums of urban decay prior to a disaster of this magnitude. Maybe now the educational system that is one of the worst in the nation would get a much-needed boost and the residents of this region would be empowered to make the transition from the sand traps of poverty to the solid ground of prosperity. We've got to understand that many people caught in the clutches of poverty are there only because they see no way out. This disaster as terrible as it was served as a way that for some who years ago saw no escape from the snare of lack.

What a challenge to consider outright devastation as a viable answer to your prayers concerning a betterment of one's life? Apart from the residents who precariously benefited from the dilemma of Katrina,

# The Dusk of Mankind and the Dawn of the Kingdom

there must have been businesses that started directly as a result of the resultant need that now existed in the area for redevelopment. I believe that we are still years away from hearing the stories of victory, recovery and transformation that will come out of this tragedy.

American history, a history of which I am keenly aware, and one that is unique in its character of being birthed in the depths of tragedy gives us an all-encompassing example of how Godly providence can be traced although not immediately evident in the background of human embattlement. In this chapter, The Great Challenge, we are asked to use the idea of belief in God to negotiate the obstacles of this life. Our lives by their very nature depend on obstacles. Obstacles give our life meaning, and they inculcate purpose, and character into who we are. If we shrink back from these obstacles then our lives will be molded around those choices that we made in fear. However, if we boldly take them on our lives will be shaped by faith.

Despite the defining obstacles of our distinct lives, there is one constant, and that is that we are children of God. Some of us may be rebellious children, or resentful children but we are children nevertheless. What does that mean for the challenge that we face? Does that mean that just because I am by origin a child of God then despite my choices to the contrary, my end is assured with Him? Or does it mean that I can forfeit that status, that assurance of being an heir of His? I believe the latter. I believe that our great challenge is to see the obstacles for what they are; learning and training experiences. When we make a bad decision, I believe that through prayer we should come back to God who set the obstacles in our path in the first place. In doing such, we then have an opportunity to ask for His forgiveness, and to explain why we did what we did and await his response.  God in turn, I believe, continues to set forth his divine purpose even in the midst of human error.

American history from the days of our country's infancy was and to some degree, still is a history weaned on tragedy and trying decisions.  The first European settlers came here fleeing the tragedy of persecution.  They set up settlements in this land but in so doing disrupted the lives of the Native Americans who already occupied this land.  Historical accounts conflict as to whether the initial encounter between the Pilgrims and the Native Americans was peaceful or not, but we do know that after subsequent years the Native American population suffered great loss.  Hence, the Native American population although diverse in their own way suffered the collective tragedy of destitution by disease or violence.  The first people of African descent forcefully brought to this land also were a part of the tragic reins that bridled the horse known as American history.  Again figures fluctuate from a few million to several million who died, were kidnapped, and were killed as they were brought here to lead lives of forced servitude.  Again the obstacles of societal advance led people to make what appear to be tragic and often even evil decisions.

Slavery was a demeaning, destructive and tragic experience for all involved and one for which mankind is yet to be judged, but I believe that it still does not prevent God from establishing his purpose in the earth.  The damage was so divisive that the vestiges of its impact are still felt by African Americans generations removed from the practice.  The societal sentiments that still cause people to be suspicious of each other's intentions based on the distinctions of color, creed and culture are clear evidence that slavery dealt a crushing

# The Dusk of Mankind and the Dawn of the Kingdom

blow to the moral fabric of the American experiment. Even in the demoralization of slavery God raised up Godly men, slaves and non-slaves who championed the ideals of human dignity and reverent fear of the Lord. These men and women used the doldrums of slavery as their catapult into purpose.

Is there a tragedy in your personal experience that you can use as your springboard into purpose? It will be painful but it will be worth it. Anti-slavery activists, abolitionists and civil rights figures all took painful steps to walk in their purpose. Most of them died without seeing the fulfillment of their life's work, but we are living today as beneficiaries of what they endured. We are living today able to pursue areas of study, work and even sports in which African Americans once suffered exclusion. The economic gains that young professional African Americans now have, be it in business, sports or entertainment are no small thing considering what the race has had to deal with in the past. It takes a Godly kingdom perspective to see the overarching future benefits that were availed African Americans even from the experience of the colonial slave trade. Again the mosaic of tragic life does not alter the purpose of God being advanced in this world. We've got to get our minds in a place to recognize the surety of that fact.

The ultimate challenge when all the chips have fallen is that of sacrificing one's life for the purpose of seeing God's kingdom come. Being able to sacrifice comfort, possessions, and peace in this existence so that God's program could be set in action is the ultimate challenge of the believer's walk. We have got to be ready to speak up and stand out for the ideals of godliness. In this world that is a position that is often rejected and ridiculed. Giving what we have in finance, as well as in dedication is something that we must do to adequately play our part in kingdom work.  Sacrificing our peace in the way of severing some relationships and losing some people's support are also ways that we can help to make his kingdom come.  Losing their support allows for God to come in and give his ultimate support.  There is no better foundation or support necessary for our sustenance than that of which Jesus Christ laid on our behalf.

### *Kingdom Keys* **on the Great Challenge**

The great challenge as reiterated throughout this chapter is the challenge of belief.  Believing God despite the chaos, confusion and distractions that life often deals us.  I am truly grateful for the fact that God never required us to fully understand him, and his ways.  In fact, he declared that his thoughts and ways are far beyond ours.  Therefore, we could stand in the assurance that our belief in Him is not predicated on us understanding Him.. The great challenge for us is to set aside the human propensity of seeking knowledge.  We're so accustomed to ascending to belief only after we've neatly comprehended every asset of a situation.  We've become so used to calculating outcomes and assessing conclusions before we truly believe that when God asks us just to believe without understanding we find it almost an impossible gesture.

The kingdom that we pursue; the government and righteous influence of God in the earth, is an experience that must be apprehended, and sometimes, with little physical evidence of its presence.  Jesus, in his response to the inquiry of the Pharisees about when, where and how the kingdom of Heaven was to be established stated, "The kingdom of God cometh not with observation."  He even concluded further that the

# The Dusk of Mankind and the Dawn of the Kingdom

kingdom of God was actually on the inside of his followers. The Bible also tells us that now faith is the substance of things hoped for, the evidence of things not yet seen. Our belief is a faithful belief. It is one that depends on the invisible but tangible promise that God has made concerning those who are His. We're heirs, joint heirs with Christ. That means that our inheritance, our portion in God's will and testament is vast. We can't see it, we may not even touch it in our lifetime with our physical hands but our very existence, and survival, and daily provision in this life is evidence that it is real.

Without faithful belief we could never see the kingdom much less enter it. We've got to fight every negative thought, and every contrary argument that society, friends or even self may develop in response to life's trials. How do we fight unbelief? We've got to feed on the promises of God. We've got to consume His Word. Just reading without personal application is merely education or enlightenment. We've got to read and pray for God's revelation and that is what will bring us empowerment. Empowering study of the scriptures fueled by regular communion with God through prayer and fellowship with other like-minded believers will take our measure of belief from the stage of elementary chrysalis-like trust to a place of butterfly-like assurance and knowledge that God has done it because your life now mirrors what you know God said.

As you wrestle with doubt, and try to corral the stallions of impulsive reactions take on the bridle of God's Word. The devil knows that belief is the final bridge that any soul desiring to come to God must travel across and therefore his entire arsenal will be targeted at preventing this crossing from occurring. Set your face against the wall, bear down and believe the Word of God and victory will be your sure reward.

# The Dusk of Mankind and the Dawn of the Kingdom

## Chapter Ten

## Living in Your Midnight

*And at midnight, Paul and Silas prayed, and sang praises unto God: and the prisoners heard them.*
                                                    Acts 16:25

    All of us at one time or the other has experienced midnight in our lives. It doesn't depend on age, social status, wealth or cultural distinctions, but rather is a universal experience. Midnight can be an occasion, or it can be a season. The characteristics of the experience for all who have been through it are the same. At everyone's midnight it's the darkest it could possibly be, and even when we open our eyes as wide as we could in an effort to increase our ability to see the effort is futile. Living in America, especially if one is a resident of its urban hubs, we tend to believe that the neon lights of the city midnight anesthetize the experience of a pitch-black night. We have the feeling that people from New York, or Los Angeles or even Vegas could never relate to a completely dark night in their lives. And this may be true in the physical sense,

## The Dusk of Mankind and the Dawn of the Kingdom

but the midnight I'm referring to is the type which fills our spirit with the sense of pending nothingness reminiscent of standing on an unlit street corner at 12 in the morning.

We've all been there, when we strained our spiritual eyes to see beyond our present circumstances into where God is leading us, or resolutely where we are leading ourselves, and we see nothing. In fact, it is so dark we can't even see ourselves. Our hands held inches away from our eyes looks no different from the nothingness that separates us from what we are and where we are, to what we are to become, and where we should be.

In the natural, midnight is a precarious time of the day. It is literally unbounded by either day or night. All other times can be clearly distinguished as either day or night. Midnight, however, stands at the crossroad of the two. It is a time of transition, a time of indistinguishable but definite change. One minute before midnight and one minute after midnight literally separates one day from the next but from all appearances nothing has changed. Have you ever felt yourself in that situation? Have you ever been going through a bout of depression and dark days hoping for some relief and with every marching day it appears as though nothing has changed?

It is in these times, in the hours of our individual midnights that God desires to purge us of the things that act as scaffolding and support for our lives outside of Him. Midnight strips us of all the things that usually would give us comfort. We take comfort in being able to see where we're stepping when its light outside. But what do you do when its completely dark all around you? During the day, in the brightness of light we don't even think about the things we reach for. We do it almost automatically because our minds have memorized where things are in our lives. But what do you do when your reach for something that you thought was there but because of the obscuring nature of darkness you grab onto something that is actually harmful? Midnight puts us in a place of vulnerability. We no longer can depend on sight. At midnight, sight loses its ability to act as insurance.

Midnight can be so enveloping and disorienting that it even alters our ability to hear correctly. The darkness of midnight collapses upon our conscience like a cloak and gives texture to nothingness. Our conscience is exercised in our moments of midnight. We sit, or stand, or kneel, or lay prostrate consciously beckoning God for answers; for a turnaround or for a breakthrough but no answers come. No other physical experience in life parallels spiritual midnight better than that of the experience of solitary confinement in a prison. Spiritual midnight is God's version of solitary confinement. It is a time when companionship is severed-a time when the assurance we gain from being in the company of others is non-existent. It is a time when God wants us to face ourselves alone.

The emptiness that we feel in our midnight season is more like a sense of helplessness. Unfortunately, many people translate that helplessness into hopelessness. However, helplessness and hopelessness do not only diverge in spelling they also diverge in definition. Helplessness is a sense of being unable to inwardly gather the energy, ingenuity and wit to get oneself out of a jam. While hopelessness is a sense of being alienated from any possibility of salvation be it from inside or out. Our midnight is designed to give us a sense of helplessness. It is designed to give us

# The Dusk of Mankind and the Dawn of the Kingdom

a self helplessness that is supposed to build a Godly patience and endurance within us. God will cause us to wait until it looks impossible so that He might cause it to come to pass, because in that circumstance there is no other person, program or party that can take the credit for your deliverance.

The greatest difficulty with midnight transformations is that in the midst of these experiences we are in fertile territory for doubting. The darker it gets, and the less things seem to change, the more prevalent is the temptation to doubt. It is at the cliff's edge of doubt that we are honest with ourselves and ultimately with God concerning our weaknesses and inadequacies. Here God is then able to move on our behalf to show Himself strong in our lives. As long as the vestiges of our own self-reliance remain, God will not come in because eventually human perception will give credit for the deliverance to your ability.

Midnight is a strategy that God uses to cause us to begin to ask the hard questions about Him. When you start to begin to ask God if he is really real, and your doubts begin to cause you to take the mask off and stand toe to toe at the throne of grace and ask why, then God could move. Midnight doesn't mean God has turned his back on you, it means he's covering you in his shadow. He's covering you so that he might strip you and make you vulnerable to Him and His power. Think of God as the potter and you as the clay and when he cups you in his hand, he's literally blocking the light out of your life and he's molding and shaping you in the darkness of his hands. This He does only to open his hands once more and allow the light to come in so that he could see if you are ready for the next phase in the process of your making.

There's no escaping midnight. It has to be lived out. We can't avoid it, or forego it but we can experience it and come out bitter rather than better. This happens when we contemplate what we've done wrong and what we can't change rather than simply giving up all conjecture and speculation to a completely able God. Giving up doesn't mean bickering about our failings while still being unable to meet the mark. Giving up is looking at our shortcomings and our obstacles, and then looking unto God for answers.

Midnight is your waiting period. It is a time that God will cause you to wait, and question who you are and why you are here. Abraham had his midnight when God promised him a son in his old age. God then caused him to wait until the promise stood in a place of doubtfulness only to deliver the promised child when Abraham was of a great age.

Your midnight deliverance comes with little fanfare. At midnight you transition into a new day almost unawares. You go through, receive your breakthrough and come out and everything appears the same. This is because everything is the same the change has taken place in you. You grow in your midnight hour. Your perception changes in your midnight hour. Lot escaped from Sodom in his midnight hour. The messengers from God ushered him and his family out of the condemned city. He was delivered from the destruction that God had ordained upon the city. It was early in the cover of darkness; everything looked the same when Lot and his wife and daughters made their escape. God sent deliverance from divine destruction but Lot still pondering his own self-reliance makes a request of the Lord in objection of what God had already said. If we read the entire account of the escape in the book of Genesis chapter

## The Dusk of Mankind and the Dawn of the Kingdom

19, we see Lot questioning God's direction and instruction. God tells him to escape to the high place, and in defiance and fear Lot offers an alternative. He asked if he might dwell in Zoar, a city that was closer to his present location. In the midst of a great deliverance for himself and those connected to him, clearly operating in the grace of God, Lot was still questioning God's ability to preserve him in the mountain. He was escaping the peril of brimstone and fiery death but yet still he feared calamity in following God's instruction rather than trusting in God to complete his salvation. This was because Lot was suffering from the residue of infected midnight thinking.

Many believers forfeit complete victory and deliverance from trying issues in their life because they have a Lot mentality when it comes to how they handle their midnight experience. God brings them to the end of themselves be it in sexual addiction, depravity in the consumption of dangerous drugs or outright exposure of harmful habits to public scrutiny and these people even after being brought out by God choose to negotiate with God concerning the next stages of their breakthrough. They negotiate over the friends that they should keep. They negotiate about how long they should stay away from the places that they once frequented and to which they can trace their addictive practices. They negotiate about the severity of their therapy and that negotiation often leads to people abridging the success that God has for them. And these negotiations are unfortunately as a result of a lack of trust in God to deliver on His promise.

Jacob had a midnight experience that stretched from his procurement of the blessing that rightfully belonged to his brother, to his eventual return home to the Promised Land. Jacob left Beersheba for Haran in a hurry and fearful of retribution from his brother, Esau. His guilt was fresh and his future was uncertain, and he knew that his brother was upset. However, when he laid down on that stone to get a much needed rest in the wilderness, he not only had a dream about heaven but he heard from God.

*And behold, the Lord stood above it, and said, "I am the Lord God of Abraham..."*
                                              Genesis 28:13-15a

Although God had spoken deliverance over the life of Jacob in the very beginning of his midnight experience he still had to go through the feeling of fear over a brother's anger and possible plans of revenge. Jacob had done wrong. Yes, his destiny of rule over his brother may have been prescribed from his birth but the actions he took, with some assistance from his mother, to urge the fulfillment of that destiny was wrong. Jacob still had to deal with the consequences of his deceptive act. Justice still had to prevail. God was then going to use the admixture of Jacob's fear and his now repentant heart to usher true change in his character. The dream that he had of the staircase going to heaven with angels descending and ascending on it was a great promise, an encouraging gesture for a foreboding next part of life when he would be tried, tested and proven worthy of his promised destiny. God took Jacob's mistakes and poor decisions, he will take our mistakes, poor decisions, and the logical consequences of those, he brought Jacob to an expected end, and he will bring us to a productive and expected end as well.

Jacob's midnight was a self-imposed, mentally exacerbated experience due to his guilt. God needed him to face the reality of the fact that all that he had

## The Dusk of Mankind and the Dawn of the Kingdom

been through negatively was meant to clean him up and cause him to see that God was running the show. God ordained his life to be so, all Jacob was supposed to do was live it out instead of trying to scheme his way to the promise.

The murky atmosphere of our midnight experience causes us many times to miss the significant opportunities for major transformation to take place in our lives. It's at midnight when some of the greatest spiritual growth takes place within us. God does the work at midnight because it serves as a camouflage for His covert repairing of us. In the midst of struggle we often wear a fallen countenance. This is because the change is painful. It is a shift from the comfortable to the uncomfortable. Therefore, we find ourselves crying more, and shedding tears, and this communicates to the devil that we have given up, or that we are defeated. However, in our midnight, as we cry God is making financial transfers, he's working out people's attitudes toward us, and he's causing us to garner favor with men. This is happening at the very same time that we feel that all is loss. Midnight is the best time for God to work on our behalf because at midnight as we are concentrating on our struggle and on how we're going to make it out, God is confounding the enemy and making our way out.

Jacob fled to Haran and became the faithful servant of his uncle, Laban. One would think that his alienation from family and his guilt about what he had done would have been enough punishment and peril for him in Haran. However, we see that his midnight extended even to his relationship with his own uncle. He worked hard for his uncle for an agreed upon wage, and through him, Laban received great favor from the Lord in the way of prosperity. The very presence of

Jacob in the household of Laban at this time placed his uncle in a position to reap benefits of having one whose life was under the hand of God.  Nevertheless, Laban took advantage of this fortune and he decided to cheat Jacob out of the wages that they had agreed would have been adequate for his labor.  Jacob fell in love with one of Laban's daughters, Rachel and sought her hand in marriage as a part of his reward for service to his uncle.  However, his uncle instructed his other daughter, Leah, to go in unto Jacob, essentially forfeiting Jacob's request made to him.  Eventually Jacob got the wife that he desired but Laban his uncle still wanted him to work some more.  Jacob was becoming rich even in the midst of deception, jealousy and envy directed toward him.  When he did eventually make up his mind to depart to go back to his homeland with his wives, children and all that he had gathered in his sojourn, Laban his uncle told him that for him to leave with all that he intended to he was claiming things that really weren't his to begin with.   His uncle had seen increase because Jacob was there and now that Jacob wanted to leave Laban, his uncle felt that he should leave just as he came.

    This was a trying midnight.  By all accounts, Jacob had a right to be concerned that God wouldn't change his situation.  He had been in this man's service for years now and he had never fully rewarded him for his labor.  Jacob had a right to doubt that he would return to his homeland with little more than his wives and children.  He had a right to feel this way because what he had done to his own brother was still fresh in his mind.  He was now even more mindful of it because God was leading him to go back but he wasn't sure if he was ready to face an angry sibling.  For all intents and purposes, despite what Laban had done to him over the years it was still a more inviting experience that what

# The Dusk of Mankind and the Dawn of the Kingdom

possibly could be coming from a brother who had several years to think about all the wrong you had done to them. But even in that midnight Jacob got a visitation from God on how to deal with Laban and ultimately he had another revelation from God when he started out on his journey on how to approach his brother.

Jacob's season in Haran was both a trial and training. He was both punished (or rather suffered the consequences of his earlier sins), and prospered in his time at Laban's house. God used his deceiving Uncle to teach him a lesson and his trying circumstances to illustrate that He could do the miraculous for us even in the face of opposition.

Some of us are in a season of midnight where nothing seems to be going right. Even when you make a concerted effort to do the right thing, alarms keep going off and you're faced with negative outcomes. You finally have a heart for commitment to a relationship and the other party decides to make a break for it. You decide to do the right thing concerning taking care of your kids, and then they begin to rebel and reject your acts of love. Remember, you're in your midnight, and whatever you're going through right now is an assignment sent to transform you. The trouble might be painful but it's part of a greater production that is ultimately for your benefit.

*Kingdom Keys* **for midnight living**

If you were just to briefly recap the experience of midnight in your mind, one would see that the main effect or the main issue of the season is that one's sight is hindered.  A major part of our sensory faculties is taken out of sync when we try to see ourselves through midnight.  Midnight is a time when we start to have notions of moral and spiritual bankruptcy.  It is when we start to examine ourselves and actually find it difficult even to do that.  Remember, everything looks completely dark at midnight.  The atmosphere has been sanitized of any light but maybe the slight shimmer of a star in the distance and that is not enough for us to see our way through.  The question now stands as to what we could do in this instance?  What could we do in our season of midnight as we await a changing of day?  What do we do to encourage ourselves when everything around us is seemingly not moving, dysfunctional and completely in disrepair?

    Physically it's impossible for me to see beyond where I stand, morally I feel as though I've messed up and I can't recover, and spiritually I feel unattached from God.  This is a time when you should do something that upsets the demeanor and the plans of the enemy.  Up to this point as the doubt and despair set in and as the activities of one's life seemed to come to a screeching halt the devil sat back and applauded.  He egged us on hoping that we would curse God.  He offered some advice such as you know why this is happening to you, it is because of what you did last year.  This peril that you are going through now is because of what you did before you got saved.  He suggests that God is unconcerned about you and frankly has forsaken you in the very hour when you need him most.

    I've come to understand that at those times in my life when the Lord seems completely silent concerning my struggle is because He's standing so near if He were to speak I would be consumed.  But He chooses to come

# The Dusk of Mankind and the Dawn of the Kingdom

near and direct me toward the way from which my change will come. Job said, "all the days of my appointed time, I shall wait, until my change comes." Job was in a season of midnight and peril and even his good friends were giving him errant advice and questioning his devotion. They knew that before them Job had always been a just and upright man, and when the peril befell him they could only imagine that he had been practicing sin in private. Midnight is the worse time for one to seek advice of those who can't relate to your convictions. At midnight, it is necessary that we get into the company and the fellowship of like-minded believers. It is a time when you hook up with and connect to those who have the same hope that you have.

Your feet might feel like they' re stuck in the mud, but as long as you make you way to the house of the Lord, you're making progress. Midnight is a season of indistinguishable progress. Your heart might be hurting. Your eyes may be tearing up and your vision may be cloudy, but if you' re aware of your surroundings enough to praise God, you're still making progress. The reason you 're going into God's house during midnight is not because of the physical structure but because of the spiritual significance of being there. We enter therein to give God the praise and to offer him our truthful worship. At midnight we've got to show God that we are serious about our convictions and that despite our current circumstances we know that they won't be our permanent situation. At midnight, my environment is unchanged and I'm still living in the same place. My credit is still inadequate, my bills still outstrip my paycheck and I've yet again been passed over for a promotion. But I'm determined to change my schedule, and rise a little earlier and work as if without me the company would collapse, but most of all I'm still present in the house of the Lord, rejoicing for what I do have and praying for what I desire.

Your goal for this chapter should be to study the story of Jacob from his birth to his eventual return to the land of promise (Genesis 25:19-33:20). It offers great insight into how we who are most of the time guilty of some indiscretion still given the possibility of redemption. It gives us insight into how we should deal with that season of feeling insignificant, and inadequate. It shows us how God can and will use our midnight to turn things around for us as long as we stick with His plans in our midnight. Paul and Silas cried out to God at midnight and they sang songs of praise unto him. They stood behind bars and restrained by stocks fastened to the cold floor of a prison cell and sentenced to silence and despair. But they decided to praise God and worship God. The Bible tells us that at midnight they prayed, they cried out unto God and sang praises unto Him and the prisoners heard. In their midnight hour, Paul and Silas used what little strength they had, what little resolve they had, what faith they had to cry out to Jesus and to pray to Him. They understood that in their situation whatever they had at their disposal was best utilized in praising God because it would eventually cause things to change. The paradox of midnight is that it is easy to give in, be cynical and just halt progress but God wants to do exactly the opposite. He wants us to keep fighting, stop choosing the mindset of failure and to keep moving. As we launch out with a kingdom psyche-equipped with a mind that recognizes the plan, purpose and program of God's establishment in the earth we are destined to encounter midnight. It has been set into the clock of mankind so as to both confuse the enemy and to recoup that which was lost. Therefore, walk it

# The Dusk of Mankind and the Dawn of the Kingdom

out in faith, challenge every fear and continue to praise God as you do it.

# Hugh J. Harmon

# The Dusk of Mankind and the Dawn of the Kingdom

## Chapter Eleven

## Advancing the Kingdom

*And now, brethren, I commend you to God, and to the word of his grace, which is able to build you up, and to give you an inheritance among all them which are sanctified.*

Acts 20:32

We are currently living in a season of great opportunity. At no other time in history has the body of Christ been this much in the forefront of world history. The believing church is slowly but surely coming out from behind its four walls and beyond its stain-glassed windows to involve itself in the debate of, and the establishment of positions, and stances on topics as diverse as poverty, AIDS, same-sex marriage, drug abuse and the politics of war. This change in the activity of churches points to a shift in the mindset of many believers from that of personal preservation to that of being mindful of the bigger picture of the

## The Dusk of Mankind and the Dawn of the Kingdom

kingdom of God. Not only is the church collective becoming more instrumental in the context of affecting societal sentiments about the issues but many of the leaders within the church have personally taken steps to use their influence with the powers that be to directly communicate the common concerns of believers so as to ensure that our voice is heard in the places where decisions are made. I might not agree with some of the positions that these self-appointed spokesmen may hold concerning the secular issues that affect churches but I do respect their assertion to take the lead and represent for the kingdom of God. This is what God is calling for us to do on our jobs, in our communities, in our families and ultimately in every place that we have some degree of influence regardless of how inconsequential it may seem.

    I heard a preacher once say in his definition of the kingdom that restoration is the plan of the kingdom, the marketplace is the program of the kingdom, and the church is the person of the kingdom. In other words, he was saying that the kingdom of God that we profess to be a part of, when we come into salvation, is threefold. It is a plan of redemption and restoration of individuals and things, a program of empowerment for us in the places where we gain our income and an integral part of who we are. We are advancing in kingdom knowledge as we draw closer to God and His Spirit dwells in us. We are also advancing through the kingdom as we possess all that is available to us and pertains unto glorifying God. And finally, we are advancing by the kingdom because our affiliation with God's elect directly makes us privilege to all the benefits of being a citizen of His coming world.

    The advancing of the kingdom is not just the job of the apostle, the missionary or the church planter but it is the assignment of every believer.  As you work out your soul salvation in fear and trembling you should be formulating ways by which your particular church or ministry could effectively change the circumstances of someone outside of its walls.  Having a kingdom agenda is essential and that does not just mean coming up with programs to meet the needs of the poor and disenfranchised in your community but involves creating programs that reach far beyond the confines of your local assembly but actually transforms a nation's thinking.  Churches should be creating formulas of aid and assistance that the world is forced to copy because they realize that the Christian model is the only one that is affective.  This is already taking place in many para-church organizations such as many of the nationally recognized prison ministry networks.  Their model of reforming prisoners through presenting the gospel and training them in the disciplines of Christianity has led to penal institutions partnering with ministries to serve as mandatory transitional centers for newly released inmates.  For almost centuries now, church organizations have led the way in garnering financial support that serves as aid for disaster victims, infirmed individuals and medical institutions.  At one point, churches led the way in the establishment of institutions of learning but after some years of opposition to the institutional practice of prayer and biblical studies the church stepped back from that pursuit.  However, today we see another rise in parochially established schools at all academic levels.  Again, the church recognizes a need that must be fulfilled not only for the children of believers but for the children of those who are still unsaved.

American secular public education as a whole is a steadily declining system of education that not only fails to adequately meet the academic needs of America's

# The Dusk of Mankind and the Dawn of the Kingdom

youth but actually oftentimes can become fertile ground for the imposition of morally questionable behavior as the social structure of some schools have become more like battlefields than places of discovery. As American society continues to develop ways to deal with the constantly shifting social composition of families and communities the issue of cultural norms becomes prevalent. America is still considered a place of opportunity and as a result, there is still an influx of new residents from very different backgrounds continually being introduced to the general and subsequently student population. In addition, to increase class size due to new foreign born admits with quite varied cultural perspectives, we have the increase as well of non-traditional family structures due to the general decay of the conventional nuclear family. Single-parent homes, less weightier moral concerns and the various other ills of overcrowded inner cities or underfunded rural districts all coalesce to create a climate in schools that fosters bullying, limited pride in academic achievement and greater concern for social acceptance. As a result, in our schools academic rigor is displaced for the greater concern of maintaining discipline, and although the standards of learning are being raised almost yearly the methods of preparation remain the same-test taking, and the outcomes continue to decline-widespread below average performance of students. How can a kingdom-minded church make a difference in a system that seems to be deeply rooted and expansive for us to have a lasting or impactful effect?

There are a few ways in which the church can change these declining trends. There are some small ways and there are some major ways that the church can help. The small ways include the examples that we as individual believers can have as educators employed within the system, parents with children in the system and as community members with a vested interest in the seeing the success of the schools that serve the community. First, the front line people, the educators working within the system have a moral obligation to be on the frontline from a spiritual perspective in prayer. The Bible says that the effectual fervent prayer of the righteous availeth much. Much of what is hindering the peace and safety on our school campuses can be dismantled through prayer. From a natural point of view, Christian educators have a responsibility to ensure that they are not shortchanging the students when it comes to academic rigor or discipline. There does not need to be an either/or scenario when it comes to maintaining properly functioning schools. Our children need discipline and they need a thoroughly challenging education or they won't be able to survive in an increasingly technologically driven and savvy world.

Parents with children in the system have a responsibility to be aware of their child's daily classroom experience. They need to be cognizant of what their children are learning and pay close attention to the changes in the curriculum especially those changes that toe the line of infringing upon your Christian worldview. Academic content should be placed under the same microscope of scrutiny that we place the material that we allow our children to view on television. If we find it offensive to watch or inappropriate to discuss at home, we should demand that it be afforded the same restriction in school. Academics cannot be simply shoved down our children's throats in the name of education. Teachers should not be allowed to teach whatever topics they deem academically inspiring because that opens the door for topics to be discussed and validated that we as Christians deem unprincipled and downright untrue.

# The Dusk of Mankind and the Dawn of the Kingdom

The more parents that actually speak up about their concerns about what they children are being taught the better the situation in our schools and our communities will get. Too many parents release their children into the hands of the school system and do not realize that they become the wards of people with their own agendas on how the world should be. What better place to set your agenda in order and what better subjects than in schools and with the most impressionable generation? We've seen this played out throughout this country with the controversy over the proposition of introducing of curriculum material that entertains tolerance for homosexuality, same-sex marriage, and the teaching and study of the Quran in public schools. Parents actively involved as volunteers in their child's school system can be great "rudders" of change-steering the ship of their child's moral preservation in the choppy seas of conformity and public pressure.

Community members that are concerned about the success of the schools in their communities also play and can play an integral part in exacting kingdom influence in the school systems of this country. Many schools are operated under the auspices of a community school district council and many times, rather unfortunately, these community school district councils are operating more like political favor machines within a given community than really being concerned about the welfare of the students in a school. Many times they are individuals who were strategically placed on these boards to ensure that the specific agenda of a legislature or a political party was fulfilled in that given district. School performance and success of the students is often the last issue on their agenda. However, these councils are meant to be independent bodies of community citizens who vote for and against policies that affect school funding and programming and many times principles and school administrators have to answer to these councils if certain programs or outcomes have not occurred. As a kingdom-minded citizen your job should be to find out how you could get involved in that council. Attend their meetings which are opened to the public, let your voice be heard and communicate effectively the mind of God concerning the district. Vote regularly and eventually you would've positioned yourself to a place of authority and influence on one of these councils. If the political establishment can do it to get their manifestos fulfilled, we can do the same because we have a Godly manifesto to win the lost at all cost.

Those are among the minor ways in which we as kingdom-minded believers can inject a mustard seed of faith into an initiative and see God cause his kingdom to come to pass through it. Those are all minor ways that if done collectively can really create a domino effect that changes the atmosphere at many of our worst schools. But as long as we sit back and become resignedly cynical we will never see change. The major way in which the kingdom church can buck the trends is for us to open our own institutions of learning and for us to financially back those that are already in existence, so as to properly equip them to deliver an education that is on par with publicly-funded institutions. It begins with churches adopting schools and making a concerted effort to raise funds that are specifically targeted to get those schools the best equipment and the best staff. It can also lead to the establishment of a network or coalition of professing Christian educators who are financially aided in their professional development by the church so that they might continue to stay abreast of educational research and best practices. There is a lot being said about unqualified and under-qualified teachers in our schools

# The Dusk of Mankind and the Dawn of the Kingdom

but we have to understand that the salaries being offered to teachers can only attract those who have less than a graduate level education. Graduate education, in and of itself, is a substantial investment of money and time for one to then be employed at a pay scale that ranks with someone with only two years of tertiary education. We've got to stop blaming the unprepared teacher if they are the only ones willing to take the meager pay that is being offered to execute a job that is a daily challenge. The only options are to spend money to prepare the teachers adequately, raise their base salaries to a decent living wage or raise teacher's salaries to be equivalent to other professionals who've had the same length of educational experience and training. If the world isn't planning on doing it, the church needs to develop strategies to do it for the well being of our own children.

The problem with the church of today is that the church wants kingdom results with mere teaching of salvation or liberation theology. What do I mean? Yes, the great objective of Jesus Christ's blameless life, eventual sacrificial death and resurrection was to save mankind from the slippery slope of sin. And yes, the message of the gospel is the message that Jesus Christ died to save us from the penalty of sin which is death. And yes, our destination once we get saved and stay repentantly covered by His blood is eventually heaven. However, what then was the use of all the stories and illustrations that Jesus gave concerning the kingdom of God if that was not something that we should also be concerned about. Jesus told his disciples at the very end of the gospel according to Matthew, that they should go into all the world and teach all nations to observe all the things that he had commanded them, including especially baptism. In the gospel of Mark it says in reference to the same statement of Jesus, that they should go into the entire world and preach the gospel to every creature. We see here as with each of the gospels that Jesus left a clear mandate to go out and spread the news of what he did and what he taught. But what actually did he teach? Was it that they should only tell of his life or were they supposed to also teach about his ideology of the kingdom? Many would take the scriptures that I just referred to and some others that relate and they would literally interpret Jesus' command as to say, "Go out and preach about what you saw me do, about why I came and about the necessity for baptism." And those believers would not be wrong for wanting to adhere that closely to what was said. However, I tend to believe that a proper handling of Jesus' message requires that we study what he taught. Why would what he did and how he live completely override what he taught? Why should they be mutually exclusive? Why should it be a either we teach salvation or we teach kingdom? Why can't we teach both?

     I believe this is one of the areas where the body of Christ today finds itself taking sides and unfairly ostracizing each other's teachings because one side or the other feels that the other side's focus is skewed. If anything, I believe one who takes sides is imbalanced and needs to understand that if Jesus did it, it was significant and if he spoke about it, it also was equally significant. This is where the rubber meets the road in the issue of today's church wanting kingdom without actually teaching it. Salvation from sin, or liberation from the vestiges of the original stain of Adam's nature is the pole mark of God's plan of redemption. However, the re-establishment of his kingdom rule on the earth through mankind as it was in the beginning via Adam is God's ultimate plan. Yes, humanity must first accept salvation and be taught the significance of the sacrifice

# The Dusk of Mankind and the Dawn of the Kingdom

of Christ but our teaching as the body of Christ should not stop at the foot of the cross but rather should advance now to the place where we see ourselves and we push others to see themselves as not just physical over comers of disease and peril, but also of poverty and disenfranchisement. The cross should be where we begin our journey to win back all that we lost in ignorance and disobedience, but it shouldn't be where we end. Again our ultimate goal should not be to obtain things or even status in this world, but it should be to re-assume our rightful authority over the things of this world. Many of us are servants of money when it should be that money serves us. We should be the agents of change in our communities but we are more like the guy or gal being shoved around as they stand in the middle of crosswalk trying to direct the pedestrian traffic, all to no avail. Change shouldn't be happening to us we should be affecting change. We are screaming repent, for the kingdom of God is at hand, confess and get baptized and live holy and you shall experience the abundant life that God promised. However, we are not explaining that there's something that takes us from being saved today, to living abundantly in all areas of our lives tomorrow. It doesn't just happen because you repented and confessed, you've got to go beyond Calvary.

This discourse literally opens up "a can of worms" when it comes to matters of theology. And as Christians eager to reach across theoretical boundaries to embrace in Christian love we often avoid discussion of these issues because of how they divide us. But as we make efforts to advance the kingdom this is a risk that we will have to take. I hope that you won't allow your denominational or personal idiosyncrasies to cause you to stop reading further. I'm not looking to create further schisms with these topics but rather I am looking to introduce a fresh perspective on what truly concerns our ultimate purpose. Just hear me out, maybe you might see things the same way I do. How do we go beyond Calvary? How do we walk victoriously in the midst of strife? How do we move from making a decision to believe in Christ and surrendering all that we are to Him, to really and truly experiencing authority over our flesh? We have to again follow the example and the instruction of Jesus. Every recorded statement or action of Jesus in his earthly ministry is significant. We should never seek to dismiss a command, declaration or teaching as being completely limited to the context within which it was spoken and to the specific persons being addressed because we can all agree that Jesus was not merely a spokesman for God but He was very God himself. He was in actuality a manifestation of God's Word. I take that to mean that he was the material representation of God's Word-the living tangible, touchable essence of God in action. Just prior to, during and after the events of the crucifixion I believe that it is especially significant that we pay attention to the Word's of Christ, and even to what transpired in the thinking of those who encountered him after the resurrection.

    Each of the New Testament gospel accounts of Jesus' last moments on the earth give added insight concerning how we should handle our journey beyond the cross. The crucifixion was the final blow in exacting victory over death. Sin corrupts unto death but Jesus' sacrifice paid that ransom completely and therefore we don't have to choose to die we can choose to live. We know this now in hindsight as we look back to the historical accounts of the day of Jesus' demise. However, for the disciples living through the experience days had gone by and it appeared that all hope was lost. In the gospel of Matthew, we understand that the

# The Dusk of Mankind and the Dawn of the Kingdom

news of his resurrection was met with doubt and outright unbelief by some of his followers. The great work of securing salvation had been completed, although this was unknown to them. Matthew tells us in his account that Jesus appeared first to the women who had first visited the tomb, and he had given them instruction to tell his disciples. These women went back with specific instructions for the disciples to go to Galilee where Jesus would appear to them. We know that these instructions came from Jesus because he had foretold the disciples this very thing would happen back in Matthew 26:31-32.

*Then saith Jesus unto them, "All ye shall be offended because of me this night: for it is written, I will smite the shepherd, and the sheep of the flock shall be scattered abroad.*
*But after I am risen again, I will go before you into Galilee.*
*Matthew 26:31-32*

The episode of peril on Golgotha had ended and with such brevity. Victory was won over sin. Death lost its sting. O, grave where is your victory? Jesus had done what had appeared to be impossible. He had made a way of escape for man from the once "inevitable" march to death in sin. But mankind did not yet know it. They had not yet gotten the revelation. Given ones perspective on the hill that fateful day, except for the period of intense darkness and foreboding that covered the land upon Jesus' utterance of, "It is finished!" the whole thing seemingly ended in a whimper. The fanfare of a coming messiah had ended in his crucifixion like the other guys that had come before claiming to be the answer.

However, this one was different. Unlike the other guys whose followers weren't forewarned and who pretty much gave up hope when their leaders died, Jesus had given a prophetic warning of what was to come and he had even spoken about what was to follow. Even with all of that some did not believe. The Adamic curse was finally broken off of our lives, and Jesus declares it in no uncertain terms and appears to us on the other side of those perilous three days but yet still some did not believe. From the first day that Jesus stepped out and declared a Word in the hearing of the people he uttered, "Repent, for the Kingdom of God is at hand!" He was echoing John the Baptist, another charismatic leader who declared a message of coming restoration but one that was not predicated on loyalty to him but on sanctity and belief in one who was to come, Jesus. Jesus came took up the mantle and began to preach repent for the kingdom of God is at hand. He heals the sick. He ministers to the downtrodden and he tells them great illustrative stories of what the kingdom of God is likened to. But only later down in his ministry almost two years in does he start to tell them about his persecution to come and his imprisonment and his eventual death and resurrection. Isn't it interesting that he didn't talk about his death and resurrection first? Isn't it interesting that the most painful part of the experience, Jesus chose to slowly reveal to the disciples? What can we learn from this?

I believe that we can learn that His sacrifice was a painful part of a greater plan of complete restoration of all things. It was a pivotal part but it was a part that was setting his people up for even more than just victory over death. Jesus was really interested in imparting wisdom to those that would have ears to hear about the nature of how things should be. Man was now embroiled in a corrupt existence heading to the

# The Dusk of Mankind and the Dawn of the Kingdom

proverbial trash heap of sin and corruption but He had come to die so that we might overcome death due to sin and live due to righteousness. Before Jesus' descent to the grave, and His offering of himself as a blameless, spotless ransom for all according to the Law, mankind really had no chance of salvation. The blood of animals was not capable of speaking out beyond the grave to save us. The lamb, goat, dove or other animal sacrifice was not efficacious enough a payment to the court of divine law. But Jesus was. He made it so that we just would not live because we had life but we were afforded life to live and declare the glory of God.

What does this all have to do with the continuing conflict among some theologians as to the preaching of liberation theology vs. kingdom theology? Some mainline denominations take the preaching of the cross as the end all and the be all of Christian doctrine. Some believe that the end result of great Christian work is to bring a soul to salvation. They believe that any preaching or teaching that reaches beyond the idea of becoming born again in Christ is basically the teaching of another doctrine. Among some more contemporary protestant movements salvation is considered a first work of grace of which they are a few more that illustrate the believers advance from being a sinner saved by grace to being a saint covered by grace. I personally believe the safest approach is to enforce the necessity of being born again through belief in the sacrificial death of Jesus Christ. We have to understand that being born again is an approach to salvation and it is not a completion of salvation. The name of the experience alone gives insight into what it is. To be born again, means that I've been given a divinely orchestrated opportunity to start over. To be born again to begin anew. I believe that this happens in an individual through them hearing the preaching of the gospel of Jesus Christ by a man or a woman of God. However, I believe that we would be doing an injustice if we were to discourage someone from seeking to have a greater revelation and experience of who God is beyond that initial decision to believe. I think it would be disingenuous for us to discourage believers from pursuing prosperity be it mental, physical or spiritual. And I believe that it would be erroneous for us as the body of Christ to amble along in these perilous times contented with the scraps that the world will ever be willing to give us, submitted to the struggles that bind us in the flesh and resolved to see heaven when Jesus returns.

After I am born again why is it necessary to pursue more of God? If our issue was our sin nature and that was now defeated by Jesus Christ's act of sacrifice, why do I need to seek more of God? We need to seek more of God because salvation from death was only the beginning. Jesus said, I came that you might have life and that more abundantly. When we are born again we are given new life, and with that receipt of new life we're also given a passport to abundance. The argument often gets touchy here when we talk about the meaning of abundance in this text. But as with other times I believe that scripture must be taken for what it says and means in the widest possible context. If God said, I've come that you might have abundance in life that means abundance spiritually, physically, mentally, socially, individually and corporately. If God is god of everything, we can't limit the efficacy of his salvation promise to just one area of our lives. We've got to apply it to all areas of our lives. We've got to apply it to our family situations, our relationships, our peace, our joy, our money and our ministry. And I believe prosperity can be had in all of these areas if we walk in the original authority that is given to us at the moment of salvation.

# The Dusk of Mankind and the Dawn of the Kingdom

The argument for anti-prosperity thinking in the church has always been that pursuit of prosperity may cause us to allow money to become our God. The statements in scripture about money being the root of all evil, as well as the pronouncement that it is easier for a camel to go through the eye of a needle than for a rich man to enter heaven, have over the years fueled the position of some with regard to the notion that God wants us to be poor. Some have even tried to use the scripture blessed are the poor in spirit for their's is the kingdom of heaven as validation of this belief that poverty was an indication of maturation in spirituality. We now know that this is not a correct summation of the aforementioned scripture but in fact, we know that the declaration was concerning a spirit that was poor in opposition to one that was prideful.

So where do we now stand? As we advance the kingdom agenda, some facts ring through. Being born again is still a necessity for salvation as Jesus Christ prescribed it. We can also agree that the kingdom of God is not just about being counted among the saved, but it is also about being trusted with power to effectively and correctly cause God's kingdom to come to pass in the world around us. If we are in agreement on those two issues, the question now is how do we move from being one who's watching the proverbial clock of Christ's return to being an active agent of kingdom implementation in the earth? Again the scriptures give the best formula for figuring out our next step in God's will. And specifically the scriptures that point to what happened after Jesus Christ's crucifixion and resurrection. The most profound and monumental incident to follow Jesus' resurrection was his ascension. If we examine the details of the events surrounding his ascension, what do we learn? We learn that Jesus left some very specific instructions on what he expected his followers to do.  We also learn that he made them some equally specific promises as to how he was going to deal with them further.

The gospel of Matthew does not mention his ascension but it does conclude with Jesus' giving instructions.  He makes a declaration, an all-encompassing declaration that I believe we as believers often forget or simply overlook.  Jesus said, "All power is given unto me in heaven and in earth."  What a profound statement of surety and authority!  We often go through life so stricken and afflicted that we forget that our God is not only powerful but He is all-powerful.  That means that if I can tap into his essence I can get the strength, the courage and the wherewithal I need to overcome every peril that this fallen world tosses my way.  This means that there is nowhere- no area, no vicinity, no circumstance in which and over which Jesus does not have the power, the authority and the rule.  He follows up that declaration with a command for them to go and teach all nations, and to baptize them in God's name.  And He concludes with a promise that He would be with them always.

*Lo, I am with you always, even unto the end of the world. Amen.*
*Matthew 28:20b*

If being born again was enough and getting on the road to salvation was enough why would Jesus feel led to promise that he would never leave them?  And how would he never leave them or forsake them if he was ascending back to heaven?  The extensively detailed gospel of Luke account of Jesus' ascension adds even more detail to what we should be expecting in the way

# The Dusk of Mankind and the Dawn of the Kingdom

of answers to these queries. Jesus promised in the other gospels that he would be a very present, help and a companion to those who believed in Him and followed his mandate. But in the gospel of Luke he follows up the promise of being with them always with another promise of sending a helper and a comforter. Jesus had served as a comfort for the disciples in their sojourn with Him. He had been a source of security, a booster to their image, and a provider of their needs. If Jesus was not going to be with them in the physical sense, any longer, they needed to get a solid assurance from Jesus. And Jesus reveals that He will be sending the Holy Spirit.

Kingdom advance must be achieved through, and by the power of the Holy Spirit. Any other source of power in this endeavor is ultimately of this world and therefore lacks the efficacy necessary to affect change from the current state of decay and corruption to that of renewal, in the world at large. The disciples had to wait on God to release the Holy Spirit into their midst. Jesus the very physical manifestation of God himself had already been among them, and his presence served the purpose of teaching those who had followed him the principles of the kingdom. However, in order for that teaching to go into effect Jesus had to remove his physical self from the picture. In the flesh, Jesus was one man capable of affecting change only in the vicinity within which he resided. But God's mandate was worldwide and even if Jesus were to personally travel to every known land at that time he still would have been unable, as a man, to spread the gospel and create kingdom like the millions who now makeup the church and are capable of doing if they worked collectively and with common purpose. The impartation of the Holy Spirit as upon the day of Pentecost was the advent of a new mode of operation of God with His people. God no longer just wanted to be with men. He also wanted to be in men. Jesus was with the original disciples in their spiritual infancy but after his great sacrificial act, the next level of the process of their spiritual maturation was for Him to dwell in them. It was then that they were fully equipped with boldness and a resolve that spoke volumes about the power of God to change men.

We want to advance in kingdom understanding and experience but we don't want to advance in our understanding and experience of the spiritual realm. The Holy Spirit and its operation in the life of a believer has often been a subject that has been dealt with in quite a vague manner by many well meaning believers. We tend to gloss over in our explanations of what we believe and our defense of the faith things that we lack a complete comprehension of. The invisible, intangible and other worldly dimensions of spiritual experience has caused many to rather loosely interpret what it means to possess the spirit of God. I remember the days of growing up in a mainline Christian denomination as a child and hearing the Holy Spirit mentioned in the recitation of the various creeds, and renditions of various hymns and songs. However, I also saw irreverence for those who praised and worshipped God with any exuberance. I grew up in a tradition that believed that the sacred nature of worship bore the necessity of corporate, solemn, silence, slow songs almost at the tempo of a funeral dirge, repetitious litanies and restrained applause at a well-delivered solo or sermon. And it was taught that the Holy Spirit was in the midst of those experiences.

I was taught that I *had* the Holy Spirit because I was a believer. But what does it mean to *have* the Holy Spirit if my life felt, seemed and looked the same way as

# The Dusk of Mankind and the Dawn of the Kingdom

it did before I made my confession?  However, on those occasions when I would sneak a glimpse into a gospel tent that made its way through our communities in the summer seasons I would witness worshippers engaged in what looked like hysterics compared to what I had been used to at my home church.  They would be screaming, shouting, yelling, running, crying, laughing and making quite a racket, as some would describe it.  And these missionaries and evangelists that would put on these gospel tent meetings in the summer would often make an appeal for those who wanted to be filled with the Holy Ghost.  Now I was thoroughly confused.  Weren't they believers and if you came to the tent and participated in all that took place wouldn't that mean that you are a believer?  And if you are a believer doesn't that mean that you already *have* the Holy Spirit and now you're calling it the Holy Ghost?  Even the semantics of the whole thing had me confused.  Was it that there was a difference between *having* it and *being filled* with it?

    The questions continued to accumulate and the dry unsubstantiated explanations that I was given, which were more like rebuttals of any exuberant practices that I had seen left me with a feeling that I would and could never truly have a heartfelt assurance of my salvation.  All of us can agree that the Holy Spirit plays an integral part in making us more like Christ each and every day and in causing His will to come to pass in the lives of those who believe in Him.  However, we diverge in our understanding and our interpretation of how the Holy Spirit influences.  Many of us were and still are believers who at one point or the other in our walk questioned whether we were saved or not.  And I believe that the questioning arose because we were rating or assessing our salvation not on spiritual things but on physical and mental changes or lack thereof that we witnessed in our lives.  Maybe it was because we began to pray more, attend church consistently, read the bible daily or even dress differently.  We may have even chosen to stop using foul language.  These were all steps in the right direction for us because they were setting precedence with regard to how we were used to living and how now we should strive to live.  But the next question was what about the spiritual side of things?

We must start where we all agree as believers.  We agree that man in and of himself is incapable of mustering enough intrinsic drive to save himself from his own corrupted state of being.  There must be an extrinsic motivation or force that causes us to seek salvation, and we understand that to be the preliminary influence of the Spirit of God in our lives.  The Bible teaches us that he literally sets up opportunities for us to come into an understanding and a revelation of our necessity for a closer relationship with Jesus Christ.  Therefore, in that sense if we do develop an urge or a desire to know God that means that the Holy Spirit is exercising some influence on you.  He has entered your sphere of reference and existence and is making an appeal for your attention.  It shows us who we really are and why we need God.  It shows us our necessity for change and the "*what-ifs*" of our continued rebellion.  And then you are brought to a place where you feel a need to do it now or else.  This is the occasion of breaking and confession.  You do it and you feel a release and a relief, and you utter those fateful, or rather faithful words, "I believe in Jesus the Christ as my Lord and Savior."  Some say this is it.  They say this is as far as the Spirit of God will encroach on our lives, it will be just an extrinsic, outer school master that will show us our wrong but won't attempt to come into us and make us.

# The Dusk of Mankind and the Dawn of the Kingdom

Unfortunately, this is also the place where many believers set up camp. They sit in the assurance of salvation from death through Christ but never seek to go after spiritual empowerment. If Jesus expected his original followers to go after spiritual empowerment he desires the same for us. Being filled with the Holy Spirit is not a casual act of a mere one time confession and pouring out of the heart. It involves us completely opening ourselves up not only to change our outward appearance and actions but most of all to change our mindset and our heart focus. We've got to get up from the foot of the cross and stop piteously lauding the finished work of Christ. Yes, the sacrificial death was a ubiquitous victory but not where we should stay in our comprehending of God's love for us and his final purpose in our lives. Jesus Christ's time on the cross and his experience of painful persecution is not to be compared to the blows that were dealt to Hell when he descended there, or to the pages that were turned in history when He arose with all power. He's no longer on the cross. He's actually seated on the throne. Some Christians have chosen to idolize Christ's defeat rather than proclaiming His victory and His continued conquering of the enemy's strongholds.

The disciples went through three days of confusion, disbelief and outright doubt. They were saved and they did not even know it. In fact, even after Jesus Christ arose and told them that all that occurred had to take place in order that scripture might be fulfilled some still did not believe. They weren't only those that did not believe but they were also those who believed but were wondering what next. Jesus, you died, was buried and rose again and now you say that you are returning to the father in heaven. We left our jobs to follow you and claim the kingdom back from our enemies but now you are leaving us without having captured the kingdom from our visible enemies. We hear you Jesus when you say that you had to die. We hear you when you say that the episodes of the last few days were a direct fulfillment of the law and the prophets. But where does that leave us? I believe that Jesus understood this to be the stance of his disciples. The gospel of Matthew tells us in the concluding verses that even after making his final appearance as according to that author of the first gospel that some still doubted the reality of Jesus (Matthew 28:17).

The what next of God was the Holy Spirit. God's kingdom will continue to be just a topic of discussion and utterance in men's prayers until they allow the Holy Spirit to breath into them and give them the dominion life that God blew into Adam's nostrils. The Holy Spirit was the spark that initiated man's work as a producer, protector and ruler in God's stead. God breathed into Adam and he became a living soul with the ordained purpose of being fruitful, multiplying the inhabitants of the earth, subduing the land and having dominion rule as an earthly representative of Christ. We can't expect to raze of the devil's kingdom in this world and initiate the restitution of God's kingdom first in the church, and then conclusively at the end of time, in the world without the Holy Spirit in us. The spirit of man lost its character of holiness when sin came in. When pursuit of knowledge in man superseded the necessity to obey God, sin entered into the picture and the spirit of man was eternally-tainted because it now was bent toward self-actualization and self-will.

We need the Holy Spirit to fill us in order that we might properly usher in God's kingdom in the earth. The human spirit can contemplate doing right and may endeavor to do good but good, as with what man considers right, is not always God. We may be able to follow routines and regimen when it comes to religion but intent and content of one's heart supersedes any religious practice because it indicates ones relationship with God. If we are intimately related to Christ we would not need to immerse ourselves in religiosity because his image will shine forth in us, religiously attired or not. The church on a whole has got to see that Pentecost is not a denominational distinction but rather is a spiritual experience that regardless of other doctrinal divergences we all should be endeavoring to embrace. A Christian that is denied the Pentecostal experience or dissuaded about its efficacy and legitimacy within the practice of foundational Christian ideology is being robbed of a full experience of the breadth and latitude of God's influential power in their lives. They will continue to fall victim to the wiles of the devil, and immersed in the vicious cycle of falling down, confession, repentance and repeated error. This is because they will simply have a heart to do right but no inner spirit force to compel them to do right, only a conscience to remind them that they are doing wrong. Let the Holy Spirit move from being just a tool of the uninvolved but alerting conscience to being a mechanism of the actively pursuing soul.

*Kingdom Keys* **for Holy Spirit Advance**

You may be sitting and saying that you are that person in that church that does not believe in the Pentecostal experience. You may have grown up in a family that saw all of that emotion and hugging and crying that is reminiscent of our kind of church as pretentious and choreographed. My family was the complete opposite we seldom hugged and we just about never told each other we love you. Therefore, my view of overt affection and utterances, of, " I love with the love of the Lord," was one of disdain. I just saw it all as a great put on. So I can definitely relate to what you may be feeling right now. You might even be one that thinks the music, dancing, shouting and running up and down the aisles in church to be too much exuberance. But regardless of your stance I want you to do a deep self-examination.

We know that much of the exuberance that we see in church today really isn't due to the in-filling of the Holy Spirit more so than a spirit of enthusiasm that is seeking relief from the drudgery of a long week. Since you have given your life to the Lord, or rather since you've started coming to church do you feel that your confession has made any real difference in your life. Think about how the disciples felt after the crushing blow by blow events of the fateful night of Jesus' arrest. Think about those who doubted even after they heard and saw him risen from the dead. Did their assurance of him being alive and well serve as enough of a "carrot" to continue with ministry? It may have served as a great point of launch and discussion when they met a prospective soul but something more was needed. The gospel of Luke and the book of the Acts of the Apostles weaves together two text and creates the fabric of one story of how God was setting His followers up to receive a great reward for their patience.

Jesus taught them about the kingdom. He taught them first about the constitution of the kingdom, the beatitudes, the attitudes that we should adopt as kingdom-minded people. Then he taught them about the actual structure and systematic operation of the kingdom through the kingdom parables. Lastly, he warned them about the end of time and of how the kingdom of God would finally be revealed in its fullness. He taught what he taught with the intent of preparing

# The Dusk of Mankind and the Dawn of the Kingdom

them to receive Him into them. He was showing them that what was to be achieved could not be done by man's strength of self-discipline but rather was dependent upon man's reliance on Him and his power. Now that Jesus was gone he had to send power, his power to sustain men. In order to fulfill that mandate Jesus sent his Holy Spirit to dwell not just amongst us but within us. Study the Acts of the Apostles, and look to understand the significance of the Holy Spirit's work in causing expansion and increase in the church in those days. It is that same spirit that desires to increase and expand the body of Christ right now through you.

# Hugh J. Harmon

# The Dusk of Mankind and the Dawn of the Kingdom

## Chapter Twelve

## Kingdom Living in a Dying World

*The kingdom of God cometh not with observation:*

*Neither shall they say, Lo here! Or, lo there! For behold, the kingdom of God is within you.*
Luke 17:20-21

*For the kingdom of God is not meat and drink; but righteousness, and peace, and joy in the Holy Ghost.*
Romans 14:17

I think it is necessary that we reiterate what the kingdom really is at this juncture in our study. The kingdom is the manifested authority of God in the earth as it is in Heaven. It is His government, authority and rulership in the spirit realm that has the ability to dictate outcomes in the physical realm. When we consider the dusk of mankind and the dawn of God's kingdom in the earth we must pay particular attention to the fact that we are called to live a paradox as it were. My life, our lives if we are children of God must contextually go against the grain of worldly demise. As

# The Dusk of Mankind and the Dawn of the Kingdom

the title of this chapter suggests we have to live while the rest of the world is content with dying.

Jesus declared after hearing of the death of John the Baptist that the Kingdom suffereth violence and the violent taketh by force. The moment we take up the cross of faith in Christ we also take up a bull's eye that makes us a target for the enemies attack. But regardless of the onslaught we have to forcefully stand on the moral ground of Christ's righteousness. The devil's only apparatus or strategy is to prompt you to go back to what you used to do. He wants you to waver. He wants you to take down from what you've come to believe and go back to living a lie in a single moment of indiscretion. He wants your mind to wander in the wilderness of lust so that you will be overcome with that temptation. And he will not stop until God intervenes. God's gives him permission to unleash his attack and therefore, he waits on God to pull his coat. The devil's desire is that you fall in lock step with the condemnation of the world, but God's desire is that you prove His glory.

The conclusion of this entire matter of the dawning of the kingdom of God is that we have to rediscover our position in God. If we are correctly positioned in God we will be able to weather the ensuing storms. Storms come in many forms it may come as words, actions or even simply as thoughts. The closer I am in my commitment and connection to God the less likely I will be distracted by the storm of words. Words have the definitive power of being able to plant seeds of dissent even in the most resolute of souls that is if we open ourselves up to receive it. As children, we had little control over what was spoken over us and even less control over what we received or not. As adolescents we unconsciously had the uncanny ability to stand as if paying complete attention to instructions, even being able to repeat the instructions verbatim but not really inwardly processing them. It got to a point that it had become a habit for us to forget just a few minutes later what had been already told to us. As teenagers it was involuntarily that we listened without hearing. But as adults we have the wherewithal to cancel negative speech over our lives. We know how to voluntarily listen to someone and not really hear them.

This is how we need to be when it comes to blocking the reception of demonic communication in our lives. Any ungodly communication can fit into the category of demonic communication. If I'm correctly positioned in God my auditory senses are so in tuned to the melody of God-to his Word and to his way that anything that is contrary to what God already said will not sit well with my conscience and I will be able to cancel it immediately. If I study scripture and determine in my mind to memorize scripture so much and so that my vocabulary becomes scripture, and I am continually repeating it in my spirit, I will not have room in my psyche for the devil's news.

Give the devil no occasion for accusation. Our salvation is a gift from God through his unrelenting and ever seeking grace. The grace of God said that man needed a savior and that savior had to be perfect while yet still being relative. God's plan of redemption had to include a formula that took into account the necessity of the fulfillment of his already concretely laid down law and the fallen state of man's nature. A fallen man that needed to abide by God's unshakeable law could only depend on a merciful God to give him a way out. Jesus was the way out. God wrapped his Word in flesh, caused it to separate from his fatherhood and come to earth to occupy and deal with the confines of human

# The Dusk of Mankind and the Dawn of the Kingdom

life. The necessity was to bring to man an example of one who perfectly abided in God's will while still being vulnerable to man's shortcomings.

As human beings we can easily say that what God expects of us is impossible because we are less than perfect. But what really is it that makes us less than perfect? Is it that we are imperfect as a creation? Is it that God made some errors when He made us? Some would argue that God knew that man would fail and fall, therefore that would suggest that he made us somewhat with a fault. Some might even venture to say that it was a deliberate act to keep us subordinate to Him. However, by the very fact that we are created beings whose existence was due to the action and purpose of another renders us subordinate just by design. Or is it that right now in the state that we are in tainted with original sin our ability to claim perfection is stymied?

The circular argument of those that accuse God for the existence of sin in the world and the general decay of human morality begins with a controversial and I believe, errant suggestion. The suggestion is that God made an imperfect man and then threw him out in the world with an expectation of perfect obedience. That argument alone would collapse the necessity for repentance of man and confession of perceived wrong, in order to receive the remission of sins. Why would I have to repent and confess for something that I really had no capacity to avoid? This is the argument of the atheist or the agnostic as they endeavor to erase God from the equation of life. They believe that God really doesn't exist, but is the creation of the collective imagination of a mankind seeking purpose to a perilous and often unrewarding existence.

## Hugh J. Harmon

The contention that God did a deliberate "messed up" job when he made man is to lend fuel to the atheistic flame. A God that makes such a monumental mistake is not a god at all, and therefore, deserves cancellation and erasure from history. But we know as believers that what God did in the seven days of creation was to establish a perfect work. The earth was perfect, the beast of the air and the beast of the field and the beast of the sea were all perfect. In fact, God called them good. And when he completed his creation of man he uttered, "It was very good!" That let's me know that if God said it's good that means it's good and perfect. It wasn't just good and finished, it was good, finished and anointed to walk in perfection.

*And God saw everything that He had made, and behold, it was very good (suitable, pleasant) and He approved it completely. And there was evening and there was morning, a sixth day.*
                                                Genesis 1:31 Amplified

What was it that made it anointed to walk in perfection? It was that God's creation at its completion was made suitable to perform its purpose. To be perfect is to be operating completely in the arena or the purpose for which one was made. A perfect bottle cap fits perfectly onto the bottle top that it was made for. Man was made for the purpose of being the expressed image and likeness of God in the earth. He was made to be the representation of God in the earth (i.e. ruler, authority, dominion) and to illustrate God-like attributes. How was he to be like God? He was to be fruitful (i.e. creative), multiply (i.e. reproduce himself), and subdue (i.e. put under subjection and control) the earth. Therefore, that means that as long as Adam operated in his purpose, he was perfect. He had no distractions. There were no other humans around. His only communication was with God-perfect. That means that he was completely abiding in God's will (i.e. being his companion) in the earth.

At this time, Adam was just as much flesh as we are flesh today but his spirit man had rulership in his life. Adam ate just like us, he slept, he worked and he rested. However, the issues of his flesh did not dominate his existence because he lived according to the spirit, and obedient to God's instruction. As he walked in the spirit God was able to clearly communicate to him what he needed to do to maintain balance in his flesh and keep his spirit open to God's voice. Today, however, we live according to the dictates of our flesh, and our spirit man's needs are secondarily handled, because we do not have as close a relationship with God as Adam had in the beginning. The order of things has been changed the issues of our flesh dominate our lives because we overfeed the flesh and it is therefore made more sensitive to need. On the other side of the coin our spirit is starved and basically kept away from its source of refreshing, which is communication and connection to God. We are not perfect today not because we weren't made perfect in the beginning, but rather because we have neglected to operate in the purpose for which we were made, and according to the mechanism that God had for us to operate.

Think of the analogy of a plastic mug with a cover, one that you might have sitting on a shelf in your pantry right now. It once was a container for juice. You bought it from the supermarket and it served its purpose of holding that juice in the refrigerator. But now the juice is gone but you are hesitant to throw the container away because it could serve as a good container to store sugar or flour. You remove the wrapper that it once had that proclaimed to the world that it was a juice container and you leave it unlabeled and pour a bag of sugar into it. You then take it and rest it on the pantry shelf. It now becomes a sugar container. That's not what it was made for but it does do the job. Whenever the sugar runs low you see that some stays stuck to the bottom of the container but instead of washing it out and discarding the container you just empty another bag of sugar in and keep using the container as a sugar holder. Many of our lives, our bodies, who we are has become like that juice container turned sugar holder. We are suitably fulfilling task and doing other things that we ultimately weren't made for. We weren't made to hold sugar, we were made to hold juice. We weren't made to become slaves to our flesh and subject to the cares of this world. We were made to rule over our flesh by allowing our spirit man to lead the way in our decisions, work and thoughts. We weren't made to seek God only in times of trouble, but we were made to seek God in all things and not through any major productions of bombarding heaven but through continual communication with him.

Jesus' job therefore was to show man how to be a spirit that lives in flesh as opposed to how they were living as flesh that had a spirit somewhere out there, a spirit that was of less significance to their existence. Our perfection depends on us not recreating ourselves through intellectual pursuit but begins with is being reborn from above. To be reborn from above is to have the old channels of communication reopened between your spirit and God's spirit, and essentially moves a step further to God's spirit actually merging with our spirit and becoming one. It involves our spirit coming under the tutelage of God's spirit. This takes complete submission to God's will and His way. Jesus came through the channels of a woman to make himself

# The Dusk of Mankind and the Dawn of the Kingdom

relative to natural man, born of a woman. He then shows that a man born of a woman is able to not be consumed with the cares of this world even down to the minutia of food and drink. The bible mentions Jesus thirsting and being hungry but it never leads us to surmise that he was panicked about that possibility.

The first stage of man's redemption was the example of Jesus' life. The next stage was the issue of the law. God had set forth law under Moses for man to abide by. These laws in essence laid out plainly what God tolerated and what was not acceptable in all arena of life especially when it came to maintaining a relationship with Him. Jesus did not only have to be made equal to a man, but he had to suffer, accept persecution and die under sentence therefore that the law that God had put in place and could not and would not reverse could be fulfilled and satisfied. The sentence and the penalty of the Law had to be fulfilled in and through Jesus Christ. First, he fulfilled the necessity of being a man. Then, he fulfilled the regulation of living holy and righteous before God. Additionally, when he was accused and sentenced the necessities of the law were once again fulfilled. Little did the Lord's enemies know that their false accusations laid before him in the court of law although false served the purpose of bringing him under condemnation. A man condemned under the law, be it, as a result of false accusations or not, had to suffer the consequences of that sentence of condemnation. Jesus sentence was death, and he took it graciously. He died.

Jesus died and the next stage of our redemption was triggered. The angels in heaven waited with baited breath because they understood that what was to happen next was the crux of the matter. If, and when Jesus arose from that posture of death after three days

He and us would be fully vindicated because it would prove that death has no victory over the righteous. Jesus' death on the cross healed us from the wounds of original sin but his resurrection saved us from the curse of eternal separation from God. That's why we can shout, "Oh, Death where is thy sting? Oh, grave where is thy victory?"

Jesus died and subsequently rose so that we can start all over again. We now have an opportunity to really live even though the rest of the world seems to be bent and content with dying. When Jesus said the kingdom of God is at hand he was saying that the key to our access was in our reach. He was the key, and in just a little while he was going to go through an experience that at the onset will look as dark as it could possibly look but it will shed forth a light in this world that will be unstoppable. The light was going to be the wild, consuming fire of the Holy Spirit urging and pushing Jesus' disciples to spread the gospel of his life, death and resurrection for all who believed.

Kingdom living is therefore having a determination to live for Christ at all costs. And we live for Christ when we accept and believe in what He did for us. Our circumstances may not look any different after we believe but the way that we look at it should. It should no longer leave us depressed. It should no longer leave us despondent. It should no longer cause us to question his love for us. It should no longer lead us to speak doubt. Our belief in Him to do exceeding, abundantly, above all that we could ask or think should give us the assurance that what we see shall change if we begin to ask Him for change. In fact, our belief should be enough that we start thinking change and God causes change to take place supernaturally.

# The Dusk of Mankind and the Dawn of the Kingdom

Jesus said, "I am come that you might have life, and that you might have it more abundantly." (John 10:10) It's interesting when we analyze the structure of this sentence. How could Jesus insist that He has come that we might *have life*? Didn't we already have life? What was it that we had, if we were breathing, eating and existing and still not having life? The word used for having is the word, *echo*, it means to possess it or to hold onto it. Jesus' proclamation was that he came so that we might grasp onto life and not allow life to happen to us. In addition, the Greek word used for life in this text is the word, *zoe*, which literally means the ability to thrive. That tells me that Jesus came not just for us to survive but for us to thrive. And He goes on to say, and that you might have it more abundantly and this time he used the adverb *perissos*, which means to have life in superabundance, in excess or to have a superior life.

Why do we forfeit the abundant life even as believers? Why do we usually fall lock step into what the world is doing even in the church expecting to get kingdom results? It is because of our familiarity. Most of our lives we've been going along trying to discover our way by trial and error. Unfortunately, we often have to go through too many errors before we find the right path. The reason we go through more errors than necessary is because we are walking according to our sensibilities. Our sensibilities are the areas that are governed by our five senses. I like to consider them the collective that we refer to as our common sense.

We adjust our attitudes, the way we communicate, and even the way we think about things, all because of what our five senses translate to us. When we sense that someone doesn't like us due to some slight shift in their body language or facial expression toward us we react.  Our reaction is then either to retaliate or to adjust our approach all in an effort to become more agreeable or less agreeable to that person depending on the relationship we desire to maintain with them.  Our dependence on what our senses tell us then causes us to pursue compromise because we soon calculate that compromise rather than commitment to a standard would be more beneficial for us to achieve comfort in this world.  We compromise on our jobs, in our relationships, in our education and in our beliefs all because of how we read the benefits to us according to our senses, and because we want to fit in.  Our lives become a constantly shifting ball of misdirection, rejection and doubt because our senses frankly are fickle.  Our senses are constantly shifting because they assume that new means better.  Our eyes tend to wander looking for a new or a different object upon which to gaze.  Our ears thrive on picking up sounds that trigger something new is about to enter our space of existence.  And we become obsessed with what our senses extrapolate from the atmosphere.  We've got to understand that the natural sequence of events in a human life unattached from a fixed point of obligation to God beyond what our senses may dictate is a life that is spinning headlong to a collision course with destruction.  Our senses are finite like our minds and they are unable to take us beyond the here and now.  As human beings we are not only dealing with what is present and evident before us but we are also dealing with that which is invisible to our natural senses and therefore we must depend on more than just our senses.  We've got to depend on God.  We've got to depend on his infinite spirit to cover and sustain us in this life.

    Our senses are lateral they keep us tied to the terrestrial.  We are limited in what we could see, hear, smell or touch beyond our physical sphere of influence

# The Dusk of Mankind and the Dawn of the Kingdom

here on earth. Hence, to live by our senses is to go through life throwing lines and hooks out at every passing whim which will eventually lead to us running out of rope. Our lives would then be stretched in every direction but up. The next step is the unavoidable onset of stress and tension in our lives. One of the most devastating causes of stress is sensory overload. It's when we try to pay attention to every changing thing and yet still focus on nothing in particular. A life separated from any obligatory reverence to someone or something more powerful than it will be a life confused, confounded and out of sorts.

Never look for victory or life in the visible patterns and trends of this world, because its victory is unplanned and happens often by coincidence and because of circumstances beyond earthly control. Our victory has to be sought in the example of our victor, our Lord and Savior, Jesus Christ. Victory without Him is short-lived, and ultimately temporarily satisfying. But if my victory comes attached to His victory, and His glory, I shall stand completely fulfilled.

The quandary in which we find ourselves is as a result of our charge as saints of God to live abundantly in a world that is determined to sustain us on scraps. Why is it that I say the world sustains us on scraps? If you look at the world from the perspective of it being not only a place but also a mindset, you'll see the reason for my conclusion. Think about it, the collective mindset of the unbelieving world is that this life is it. After this life is over there is nothing else. They also believe that if this life is it, then there is no need to believe in a God. If there's no need to believe in God then one needs to depend on their own strength, ability, and cunning to navigate the challenges of this life. Therefore, my success in this life will depend on my ability to outweigh, outmaneuver and outplay everyone else. Only the fittest will survive in that kind of a world. In addition, it would be a life in which we get nothing back for our labor unless we happen to be the biggest or the greatest. What a sorry life it would be if only those who were big and bad were successful? Those of us who didn't really add up would have to settle for what everyone else has left over. That means that I would be depending on the little that the world had to give me and not on the great that God has placed at my disposal.

Unsaved humanity has one of two mindsets either they are striving for independence or they are hopelessly dependent on others for approval and acceptance. We lose in life and end up on the side of persecution and hurt because of who we're depending on. People will always disappoint us. But God will never let us down.

The devil got us good, just a few years ago. We lost some battles, and some dreams of ours died. But, I've come to an understanding that everything that I lost in my season of maturation was meant to put me in a place of leaning on God. Every crutch that was kicked out from under me forced me to put my confidence in God. Every kick was a lesson in leaning. And as I leaned I learned how to be humble. I learned how fragile my faith was. I learned how to lose a battle without losing the war. The most productive part of our leaning is when we have to lay down everything on our last leg and accept that all of our intellect, cunning, strength or stature will not be enough to sustain us. When we surrender everything to God and hope and believe that He is able to make good out of what has become a rotten situation. It's when you get to the place where you finally accept that you have to change. In order to live in this dying world you've got to be

# The Dusk of Mankind and the Dawn of the Kingdom

capable of change. You're not mature until you can accept the fact that you are malleable. If you're still crying out that you can't help being the way that you are and you can't be changed that's an indication that you're still immature.

In order to be the greatest, we have to be able to adjust to a vacillating environment. The tides are always shifting and this world is continually in flux. Great men and women of God have shown the ability to adjust to the shift. Ability to adapt to the shift is a key attribute of one that has a spirit of endurance. And a spirit of endurance is what gives us the wherewithal to live while everyone else is comfortable dying. Many of us forfeit a good fight with the enemy of our souls because we give up in the early rounds. You've probably never heard a preacher say this before but sometimes you are going to lose. The real issue isn't did you lose, but rather what is it that you lost. Never lay all your chips on one fight or one battle because you were left laying on your back, with some bruises and bumps. If you are able to open your eyes, look up, and still realize that you are alive you have another opportunity to win. Great bouts between world renowned boxers often become sequels. Why? It is because people have realized that just one fight between the top contenders is not enough. This is why we have part four and five bouts between world class boxers. Each one knows that their chance to win is just a matter of changing their training strategy or changing their fight strategy the next time. The ones that come out of these rivalries and are finally crowned the king of the ring is often the one that was able to stand after everyone else had fallen.

To live in this world the way God wants us to, is to be great. You've got to be a great over-comer, a great defender, a great persuader, and a great convincer because without these traits you will be consumed by this world. I heard it once said that greatness is not measured in accumulated strength, power or stature but rather is determined by one's ability to correctly wield these possessions. You have also heard it said that someone with a poverty mindset if they were awarded a great fortune would find a way to get rid of it and if not get rid of it they would still assume a position of poverty. It is the same way with the greatness that God puts inside of us through salvation in His Son, Jesus Christ. We squander the deposit, the advantage that it gives us by continuing to adopt a passive worldly attitude of things happening to us rather than we making things happen.

To live in a dying world one must get desperate about survival. We have to get desperate about the promises that God has made unto us. And in getting desperate we push, press and reach for the things of God. And there's something about desperation that gives us added endurance. It causes us cling to that which restores and sustains. Once we touch a branch, or get a firm grip on that lifeline the enemy will be hard pressed to separate us. In fact, the Bible says that nothing can separate us from the love of God. When I'm desperate for anything I want that thing now. Therefore, nothing can separate me from my pursuit. I want the more of God now and I am not scared to lose other things in order that I might get it. If I'm drowning I'm not concerned about the fact that my clothes are wet. I'm just desperate for air. If I'm starving I'm not concerned about the appearance of the food, I just need nourishment. If I'm disease-ridden and dying, I'm not concerned about my finances or my job, but I'm just desperate for my healing. I have noticed over the years with the rising phenomenon of cancer that many of the people being diagnosed with this disease have also

# The Dusk of Mankind and the Dawn of the Kingdom

become the ones most knowledgeable about their disorder. Most cancer patients are urged to and develop an inner drive to educate themselves about the disorder. Personal desperation has driven cancer patients to educate themselves far beyond even some medical professionals concerning the origins and causes of cancer. They want to know where it came from, what caused it, what are the statistics on death by this disease, and their own probability of dying. When it comes to God and salvation, we have to adopt the same mentality. We have to get desperate.

Sin, the world and the devil had us on the proverbial ropes of life. We thought our recovery was impossible. After the divorce, the abuse, the drugs, the conviction and even the abortion we'd given up hope but we heard a Word of recovery and restoration. Some of us heard a young man say that he went through it but God. Others heard a young woman say I used to think like that but God. A mother declared even after he left I never needed for anything because of God. A father declared that he would become the father that he never had because God had been like that to him. Moreover, we develop a spirit of desperation, a spirit of pursuit and a longing for renewal.

Living against the grain and against the ever progressing advance of death all around us requires one to develop not only a spiritual desperation but a refusal as well. We need to develop a refusal to settle for less than what we've dreamed of having and what we've dreamed of being. I see my life today as worthwhile, but before I was saved I found it hard to muster any concept of my worth in the scheme of things. This is the attitude that births the sentiments of suicide and masochism among both young people and adults in this world. We go about a large portion of our lives seeking to find value in ourselves, our purpose and our place but we use the wrong tools to measure that value. We use the tools of this world, the material possessions, the fame, the popularity, the ability to manipulate, impress or intimidate and we fail to see that our worth is not in what man says, how man feels or how man looks at us, but rather is in what God said from the very beginning. Therefore, if we never get an opportunity to hear what God said, we end our search short of an answer, disgusted with what we perceive to be our curtailed lot in life, and we choose to live recklessly.

All of us need an encounter with God, and frankly I believe we all get that encounter early and late in life. However, I think that we then are given the option through free will to make that encounter count as a time of change or as a time of solidification in our already dysfunctional mindset. The unfortunate reality of human character is that it often has to be placed in a position of perceived hopelessness before it recognizes a need for or even makes an attempt toward seeking God. For some of us, in fact, most of us gut wrenching, heart twisting, adversity was what it took for us to change our perspective on the idea of God. Then in afterthought when we do get saved we realize that the reason our life was as disruptive and decadent as it was before salvation was because an adversary saw something worthwhile in it that he was determined to stamp out early. If I could discourage this young man or this young woman early enough they will never attain to the place that God has ordained for them. They will ultimately cause their own demise. Why would the devil work so hard to make me think that I'm nothing, persuade me to be a menace to society and blind my thinking enough to believe that no one loves me anyway, if who I am and what I possessed was of no worth?

# The Dusk of Mankind and the Dawn of the Kingdom

Adversity, especially after salvation, made me change my perspective on life. This was because I had new information about who I was and that new information gave me a greater appreciation, respect for and longing to see who I should become. I saw that my destiny was a threat to the adversary so I had to live. We've got to raise the threat level on the enemy of our soul. We've got to do exactly what he doesn't expect us to do. Rejoice when we should be crying. Thanking God when we seemingly have nothing in our hands to be thankful for and sowing seeds of hope into someone else's life especially when we need great help. Do the unexpected and God will do the miraculous.

Most of our pain in this life is based on the paradigm from which we stand and survey our lives. Our paradigm is a collective definition of how we think, see, feel and respond to the changes, challenges, and charges that life sends our way. If I'm still hurting because of what others said about me, I need to have a paradigm shift. If I'm still working outside of my field of expertise, complaining about my condition, stressed and scared to step out because of fear of failure, I need a paradigm shift. If I'm still feeling or even more so seeing myself less than God says that I am, I need a paradigm shift. If I'm still living tied to the whim and fancy of a user and a loser, I need a paradigm shift. If my paradigm shifts, I cannot lose this time around.

What difference does the paradigm shift make between now and the times before? The difference is that the last time I depended on my strength, skill, intellect and resources. The last time my strength was temporal, my skill was inadequate, my intellect was lacking and my resources fell way short. However, when I decided to shift my paradigm to that of one who was born again, saved by His blood and walking in the confidence and encouragement of His spirit, I locked into His omniscience so my intellect was unparalleled. Additionally, I locked into his omnipotence so my power source was undrainable. My entire focus and support shifted from me to God through Christ so I could not and cannot help but to win if I continue to seek Him.

God is no respecter of persons but He is a respecter of principles. He does not arbitrarily show favor to some and willfully neglect the needs of others. His favor is always tied to His divine purpose. Therefore, it's not about who I am but it's about what I am working with. What am I bringing to the table both in the tangible and the intangible? What am I carrying in my heart? If we do right, God will make our challenges come out right. Challenges are an inevitable part of our existence. If we're living saved or dying an unbeliever challenge is an experience that we will face. That tells me that regardless of my rendezvous with righteousness, regardless of my avoidance of evil, trials shall come. But if I undergo a paradigm shift those trials will become tests, those challenges will become agents of change and those setbacks will be setups for victory. My skill, my intellect and my fortune may bring me worldly advantage but it will not exclude me from spiritual challenge. Wealth, popularity and the ability to intimidate your peers often puts us in a place called pride.

Striving to live in a dying world can sometimes cause us to develop a level of pride that is injurious to our testimony. There is nothing wrong with being proud of a job well done or a life well lived, but the problem develops when our pride turns to us being prideful. We become prideful because we become acutely aware of and familiar with the sensation of

# The Dusk of Mankind and the Dawn of the Kingdom

success. Success fuels pride. Success in a particular endeavor or project, in its own way, can be an indication of purpose. Therefore, we get caught between the love of success and the pursuit of identifying our purpose. It in the miry clay of these two experiences that pride is fostered. We must learn to live with an expectation of success, having pride in our achievements but always cognizant that our achievements were all part of God's wonderful grace toward us.

King Jehoshaphat, one of the king's of Judah, who became king at a time in Israelite history that could have been categorized as the dark age of apostasy is a good example of one who had the opportunity to lean on pride and pat himself on the back for the wonderful things he had done during his reign but he never lost sight of the fact that God was the one that made all of his successes possible. His record said that he had defeated all the enemies within Israel. The scriptures in 2 Chronicles 17 tell us that he walked in the first ways of his father David. He sought the Lord, walked in His commandments, and not after the doings of Israel. As a consequence the bible goes on to say that the Lord established the kingdom in his hand. The Lord honored his obedience and his reverence and King Jehoshaphat gained riches and honor in abundance in return. In the same chapter around the sixth verse it says that Jehoshaphat's heart was lifted up in the ways of the Lord. From our contemporary understanding of that phrase we might assume that it meant he was walking in pride. However, deeper study of the term would show that it means that he was encouraged or gathered courage in the ways of the Lord. Why am I going on and on to describe Jehoshaphat and how he became exceedingly great in the eyes of the Lord?

His life and the story of his rule give us insight into two areas. It teaches how to deal with success as we endeavor to live in a dying world, as well as it teaches us what we should avoid as we find ourselves attracting success. What does his testimony have to do with us and keeping ourselves from being overtaken with pride? As wealthy and famous as Jehoshaphat became as King of Israel he never forgot to seek the counsel of God in his endeavors. He not only never forgot to seek God's counsel he also always assumed a posture of humility that genuinely saw that it was grace alone that got him the victories and success that he had. Episode after episode of his life saw him going before the man of God or the prophet of God to receive instruction on every venture. These were the right things to do. However, his story also includes an unfortunate alliance that Jehoshaphat made. This was an alliance that ultimately could have marked the downfall of his rule in Judah. However, I believe because of his record of devotion to God and to the things of God he was spared from harm. He made an alliance with Ahab. Jehoshaphat made an alliance with an unbeliever. This alliance ultimately turned into a pact to war against the Syrians. This was a war that was long overdue and a conflict that Israel brought on itself, because they had failed to annihilate the enemy in the land as God had instructed on their entrance into the promise.

Just like today, the world around the Israelite people was dying in apostasy and idolatry and pagan worship and these chosen people of God were given a mandate that before they could fully occupy and have rest in the land they would have to destroy those who already resided there. Unfortunately, some chose the path of least resistance and made treaties with these enemies rather than destroying them and these enemies

# The Dusk of Mankind and the Dawn of the Kingdom

soon became a thorn in the side of a disobedient Israel. Despite all that God had brought Israel through and regardless of how far He had brought them from, they still chose to proceed with their lives contrary to what He had instructed.

All God needs for some of us to move from surviving to thriving in this world is for us to follow His lead. God knows what we've been through and knows what's best for us. Just that simple concept is one that believers wrestle with understanding because they find it hard to believe that there's someone that knows better than them, what's good for them. But if we ascribe to the belief that God made us then who better to guide our progress but the maker? Unfortunately the old man of sin, the man tied to Adam has his own impression of how life should be lived. He has his own idiosyncrasies such as depending on his own intellect and strength. Those things sustained him in the past so a gospel that teaches that we cannot help ourselves, and we need to depend on God, rather than seek independence on self, is a hard pill to swallow. Too many of us mess up our exodus experience because we don't let our old man, and our past feelings die in our Egypt. We come out of our Egypt grudgingly. We follow orders because everyone else is but we keep our desires for the past in tact. We give up womanizing because we are fearful of AIDS, and because we like the honor that's heaped upon us for it—because that's just another injection of ego juice. But the moment our new walk gets difficult, we mutter and ponder about the past. We starve our old man for a season and we make a temporary, conditional commitment to God. But how many of you understand that discipline is not deliverance.

When God told Israel to prepare for a quick deliverance and exit out of Egypt, he gave them some very specific instructions. They had to sacrifice something valuable, and sprinkle its blood on the doorpost. There has to be a death, and a burial in your past that you don't attend. There has to be a separation from former things that seals your fate and initiates your faith. Most of us are hoping and praying for a quick deliverance. We've been dealing with setbacks and troubling circumstances in our lives for years and for some of us those situations only elevated in intensity after we got saved. It's like if the enemy has turned up the heat in your life. You've been trying your best, with all your might to live saved, and trust God despite the peril. However, before we can truly live there's some more dying that has to take place.

As I come into the knowledge of God my initial experience is strange and causes me to tiptoe into my future because I still have the residue of fear and frustration dripping off my shoulders. But after I moved forward in fear pledging that I had nothing to lose-God commended my faith, and gave me a greater revelation of Him. I saw the bush burning but it wasn't consumed. I moved from believing that God could do it, to knowing that He has done it.

We have God's spirit in full measure but we limit its efficacy by doubting its unlimited power to transform our lives. Kingdom living requires coming before God open enough to hear him, empty enough for him to pour some more of who He is in us, and weak enough to need a refueling of His power. If I'm filled with the nourishment of this world-the fame, fortune, and food of pride-I will never be able to wield the power of his kingdom, even if I possess it. This is why Jesus' disciples were unable to cast the demon out of the

# The Dusk of Mankind and the Dawn of the Kingdom

young boy. They had the power but they were attempting to wield while filled with fascination at what *they* could do. They lost sight of the simple truth that *they* could do it only by His power and in His name. When I'm weak he's made strong, and his Spirit working through me operates at full tilt.

If you sit where you are right now, and you have made it to the end of this book, and you believe in God. If you are a saved, born again believer you have a great promise. I trust and pray that if you aren't, that you would make the decision today. Jesus Christ died that we might live. And He sent His spirit to live with, among and in us that we might not just survive, but that we might thrive. Don't settle for less. The age of man's reign has drawn to an end. The great day of our Lord is upon us. There's a great light that's about to break through the passing dark. Don't wait until it is too late. Trust God now and take your rightful place at His side, reigning and ruling in His kingdom that has come.

# Hugh J. Harmon

# The Dusk of Mankind and the Dawn of the Kingdom

He lives in us that he may come through us, and impress, influence and impact the lives of those connected to us, both saved and unsaved. Fear and anxiety are acts of coming into agreement with the adversary. Faith and expectation are acts of coming into covenant with our Majesty.

Other Books By Hugh J. Harmon

# Hugh J. Harmon

Bridging the Gap: *Reconciling the ruptured relationship between man and His ever-reaching God.* (172 pages) AuthorHouse
**ISBN-10** 142591196x, **ISBN-13** 978-1-4259-1196-6

"Bridging the Gap" is a discourse on restoring civility to a life that is seemingly out of control. It is a clarion call for us to get back into right relationship with God. Man's life is a relentless search for purpose, what is our purpose, why is our purpose and for whose purpose were we tossed into this tempest known as life.

---

Of Gods, Giants and Icons: *in a world of mortals.* (180 pages) Publish America
**ISBN-10** 1424148693, **ISBN-13** 978-1-4241-4869-1

Are you an ordinary man faced with the extraordinary challenges of being a father, a husband, a role model and a leader? Has life been a series of unexpected obstacles that you weren't prepared to face? Maybe you thought you knew what it took to be a real man, but now you're confused.

# The Dusk of Mankind and the Dawn of the Kingdom

Worthy Art Thou. (108 pages) Kingdom Book & Gift LLP
**ISBN-10** 0615152813, **ISBN-13** 978-0-6151-5281-3

Have you ever thought of how much God was worth? Have you ever hazarded a guess of how much you are worth? The idea of calculating the worth of God is one that may be accounted as sacrilegious. Man attempting to assign a value to the person of God, think of it, what a travesty! of a suffering saint. How much is your belief in God worth?

---

Broken, just to be made new. (134 pages) Kingdom Book & Gift LLP
**ISBN-10** 0615163215, **ISBN-13** 978-0-6151-6321-5

*"Broken, just to be made new"* is a thesis on the often avoided topic of brokenness. It addresses the issues that lead to it and the questions that arise concerning whether it is a method used by God to mature us or a tool of the devil to defeat us.

---

For additional ministry resources by Pastor Hugh J. Harmon, or for other publications by Kingdom Book & Gift LLP, please contact:

# Hugh J. Harmon

Kingdom Book & Gift LLP
PO Box 291975
Columbia, SC 29229
(5515 Shakespeare Road, Ste 320-330
Columbia, SC 29223)
803-PEN-2472
(803-736-2472)

www.kingdombookandgift.com
www.lovefellowshipkingdomrestorationtabernacle.org
Blog Pastor H. Harmon @
www.myspace.com/fromrebel2righteousness
Pastorhughharmon@gmail.com

www.ingramcontent.com/pod-product-compliance
Lightning Source LLC
Chambersburg PA
CBHW020752160426
43192CB00006B/317